What Your Colleagues Are Saying . . .

"Shirley and Hargreaves have written the right book at the right time. They bring the voice of reason to the current heated 'culture wars' and battles over 'identity politics.' If we heed their wise counsel, we can learn to listen to one another and forge a collective identity of respect."

–Diane Ravitch
Former U.S. Assistant Secretary of Education
and President of the Public Education Network

"This essential book shows how all educators can and should address issues of identity in their schools with candor and civility. Carefully researched, it offers a clear conceptual framework and practical guidelines that can be followed in all schools everywhere."

–Patrick Tutwiler
Secretary of Education, Massachusetts

"Shirley and Hargreaves call for universal inclusive education that promotes dignity, generosity, and self-determined learning. They advocate for education that truly values and understands every individual, noting that what is essential for some children is good for all of them."

–Dame Alison Peacock
CEO, Chartered College of Teaching
London, England

"This is an excellent book and one that I will purchase for all our central leaders and school principals. It moves from academic theory to a real-life practical guide with stories that humanize our students, school staff, and communities."

–Tom D'Amico
Director of Education,
Ottawa Catholic School Board
Ottawa, Ontario, Canada

"We find ourselves in a time where being inclusive and welcoming to all students is a political issue as opposed to a human one. Shirley and Hargreaves engage readers with their collective brilliance and heart to offer clarity in thought and action to ensure that students thrive, regardless of how they identify."

Author, Leadership Coach

"This book will help us figure out how to name, interrupt, and educate when students experience anything that does not help them feel safe, included, respected, and cared for. It gives educators practical tools with which to lean into the difference between intent and impact."

–John Malloy
Superintendent, San Ramon Valley Unified
School District
Danville, California

"This is a work of courage and truth in the midst of a world that can be challenging. The content of the book fills my heart."

–Nicola Ngarewa
School Principal and Former Chair of the Teaching
Council of Aotearoa
Wellington, New Zealand

"Incisive, insightful, and inspirational. Shirley and Hargreaves present a compelling argument for schools and educators to work with students on the issues of identity. Moreover, they present practical and evidence-based guidelines that can be implemented in schools."

–Yong Zhao
Distinguished Professor of Education,
University of Kansas
Lawrence, Kansas

"Every child needs to feel that they belong in order to feel safe enough to learn. *The Age of Identity* is an inspiring antidote to school systems that measure children with standardized tests. This compelling book is an overdue dose of radical common sense."

–Jim Knight
Member of the UK House of Lords and Former UK Schools Minister

"This brilliant and profound book is at the heart of education across the globe. Shirley and Hargreaves show how learning triumphs over ignorance when students are confident in who they are. They provide teachers with tools to navigate confidently one of the most controversial topics in education today. *The Age of Identity* is essential reading for all teachers."

–David Edwards
Secretary General, Education International
Brussels, Belgium

The Age of Identity

Who Do Our Kids Think They Are . . . and How Do We Help Them Belong?

Dennis Shirley

Andy Hargreaves

FOR INFORMATION:

Corwin

A SAGE Company

2455 Teller Road

Thousand Oaks, California 91320

(800) 233-9936

www.corwin.com

SAGE Publications Ltd.

1 Oliver's Yard

55 City Road

London EC1Y 1SP

United Kingdom

SAGE Publications India Pvt. Ltd.

Unit No 323-333, Third Floor, F-Block

International Trade Tower Nehru Place

New Delhi 110 019

India

SAGE Publications Asia-Pacific Pte. Ltd.

18 Cross Street #10-10/11/12

China Square Central

Singapore 048423

Senior Acquisitions Editor: Tanya Ghans

Content Development
  Manager: Desirée A. Bartlett

Senior Editorial Assistant: Nyle De Leon

Production Editor: Tori Mirsadjadi

Copy Editor: Melinda Masson

Typesetter: C&M Digitals (P) Ltd.

Indexer: Integra

Cover Designer: Scott Van Atta

Marketing Manager: Morgan Fox

Printed in Canada

Library of Congress Cataloging-in-Publication Data

Names: Shirley, Dennis, 1955- author. | Hargreaves, Andy, author.

Title: The age of identity : who do our kids think they are . . . and how do we help them belong? / Dennis Shirley, Andy Hargreaves.

Description: Thousand Oaks, Califiornia : Corwin, 2024. | Includes bibliographical references and index.

Identifiers: LCCN 2023030940 | ISBN 9781071913130 (paperback) | ISBN 9781071913154 (epub) | ISBN 9781071913161 (epub) | ISBN 9781071913178 (pdf)

Subjects: LCSH: School children—Psychology. | Identity (Psychology) in children. | Belonging (Social psychology) in children. | School environment.

Classification: LCC LB1121 .S55 2024 | DDC 155.42/4—dc23/eng/20230814
LC record available at https://lccn.loc.gov/2023030940

This book is printed on acid-free paper.

MIX
Paper from
responsible sources
FSC® C103567
www.fsc.org

23 24 25 26 27 10 9 8 7 6 5 4 3 2 1

Contents

Who This Book Is For

This book is written for the vast majority of educators, families, school board members, and everyone else invested in education. It speaks to everyone who wants their children—and, if they think about it for a moment, other people's children—to succeed, be well, and belong. It appeals to all of those who sometimes feel that they themselves are treated unjustly, unfairly, and unkindly, as they try to do what's best for kids.

It's a book that strives to get past the culture wars and the more volatile aspects of identity politics that divide communities into villains and victims, or aggressors and aggrieved. It moves beyond treating each other as singular, oversimplified, and often stigmatized identities. It rejects the ways in which people feel they are portrayed, and sometimes pilloried as one-dimensional beings, defined by or demonized solely because of their race, disability, privilege, or gender identity.

Our book urges readers to honestly confront exclusion and oppression wherever it exists within and beyond our schools. Yet, it also moves beyond discussing what to do about these injustices in languages of accusation, indignation, guilt, and shame.

Identity issues affect all of us and are the responsibility of all educators. What kinds of people children are and need to be now and in the future is at the heart of child development, of moving through adolescence, and of entering the adult world. Identity issues and even identity politics aren't just about particular groups, or other people, of one kind or another. They concern all of us.

Identities are also multiple and complex. All of us are many things, not just one. We may see ourselves and each other in terms of our race and ethnicity, our gender identity, our nationhood, or our stage of life. Other, less discussed aspects of identity may include our line of work; being a twin, a mother, or a grandfather; being a cancer survivor; or having a passion for marathon running, cooking, or musical performance.

> [This is a book that] rejects the ways in which people feel they are portrayed, and sometimes pilloried as one-dimensional beings, defined by or demonized solely because of their race, disability, privilege, or gender identity.

To treat and categorize people in relation to just one aspect of their identity, however important, even where we mean well, is an insult to their dignity as full human beings. It turns people into boxes to be ticked or adversaries to be defeated. We must strive to understand our kids as whole beings, in all their complexity, with many changing facets to who they are and what they might become. Appearances, especially first appearances, can be deceptive. What we see isn't always what we get.

We want this book to inspire readers to address not just what should be attacked, opposed, canceled, or removed, but also, and mostly, what can be done together. We envision a time when dynamic communities of rich diversity will create success, fulfillment, inclusion, and belonging for everyone. In this quest, it's important to appreciate we are all imperfect and make mistakes from time to time. None of us has all the knowledge and all the answers. Humility is a necessary milestone on the road to humanity.

When we get down to it, in practical everyday language, we will appreciate that what is essential for some groups of our kids will usually benefit all of them—safer schools, a richer and more engaging curriculum, and more diverse pools of skills and talent. We will all get to know each other better and will accomplish more together. We will find ways to discuss disagreements and differences in a spirit of goodwill and with a mindset of civility that respects and protects one another's dignity.

This is what most people want. Those very few who believe they have nothing to learn from their opponents, and who engage in culture wars and identity politics to advance their self-interests, or to distract their rivals, are not the people for whom this book is written. For everyone else, let's begin.

Preface

Education and Human Development

This is a book about one of the most abiding aspects of education and one of the most compelling and controversial issues of our times: identity.

Since schools were first founded, from the ancient Greeks onward, education has been about more than accumulating knowledge and skills.[1] It has addressed how to develop people and help them form their character, and how to shape whole societies and civilizations. From its Latin origin, *educere*, education is not about drumming ideas into people. It is about leading people and their ideas out.

The Catholic, Jesuit tradition, in institutions like our own Boston College, is dedicated to education as a process of human formation.[2] The German and Northern European philosophy of *Bildung* imbues public education with a spirit of self-cultivation and unifies identity and the self with the broader society.[3] Culturally responsive teaching addresses how the content of the curriculum should enable students from diverse backgrounds to feel like they are included, engaged, and belong in their school environment.[4]

In virtually every country, education contributes to nation building by cultivating belonging among young people, through developing their sense of collective identity. The International Baccalaureate and the British Commonwealth's Duke of Edinburgh's Award program both include service to the community as a significant part of their curriculum. With threats to democracy, to voting rights, and to the privacy of voter information, educational systems in many nations are also rediscovering the importance of making democracy a central part of young people's experiences in school.

Who are we? What will become of us? What can we be part of? How will that make the world a better place? These questions are fundamental to how people experience education. In the words of the classic French

> Who are we? What will become of us? What can we be part of? How will that make the world a better place?

sociologist and former teacher Émile Durkheim, education shapes the generations of the future. Many teachers today still recognize the truth in the old dictum that they don't teach subjects, they teach children. Parents want their kids to succeed. But they want them to be happy and fulfilled too.

By design or default, identity is always integral to education. We can't avoid it, even if we try. In the four decades spanning the turn of this century, though, it looked like the world was making every effort to subordinate identity and human development to the global drive for increased economic performance and educational achievement. Identity issues were overlooked and ignored. They were rendered invisible.

From Achievement to Identity

From the 1980s onward, more and more schools and school systems were thrown into what we have called an *Age of Achievement and Effort.*[5] Educational policies reflected priorities to bring about more and more economic growth, as measured by gross domestic product, rather than focusing on sustainability and quality-of-life factors such as happiness, meaning, purpose, inclusion, and sense of belonging. Performance measures in education mimicked performance targets in economies. Education policies were defined by efforts to drive up standards, narrow achievement gaps, outperform competitors, race to the top, benchmark against the best, spend more time and effort on formal learning, deliver measurable outcomes, and improve results.

At first, some of these measures gave needed direction to school systems. Before long, however, they took on an unstoppable logic all their own. Many important aspects of human development were sacrificed to the lemming-like rush toward the cliff's edge of never-ending achievement gains. Preparation for competitive tests and examinations left little or no time for arts, social studies, physical education, or learning outdoors. A vast industry of cram schools and grind schools grew up, along with other private tutoring services after school. Homework increased. Student engagement suffered. Anxiety and other kinds of ill-being began to affect young people's mental health. In the *Age of Achievement and Effort*, identity issues were officially irrelevant.

Things started to change from about 2010, though. A new age emerged of *Engagement, Well-Being, and Identity.* Our book is one of three we have written on each of the three parts of this age.[6] This one is concerned with the *Age of Identity.*

From 2009 up to 2018, we undertook two long spells of working with a representative sample of 10 of Ontario's 72 school districts in a consortium to analyze and advance the agenda for inclusion that they had been asked to move forward by the province's Ministry of Education.

Inclusion was originally a more sophisticated way of thinking about how to support children with special educational needs. It was about shifting from an emphasis on legally and psychologically identifying individual children with exceptionalities and providing interventions and supports for them, to creating environments where collaborative teams of teachers used differentiated instruction with the assistance of technological supports that could enable all students to succeed.

From 2014, under a new premier, Kathleen Wynne, for whom Andy was an education adviser, the province, and, therefore, the 10 districts in our consortium, deepened the approach to inclusion, equity, and well-being. Excellence was defined broadly beyond literacy and mathematics to make the school "a compelling, innovative and engaging place to learn for all students." Equity was about "inclusivity and respect," "regardless of ancestry, culture, ethnicity, gender, gender identity, language, physical and intellectual ability, race, religion, sex, sexual orientation, socioeconomic status, or other factors." Well-being would promote "a positive sense of self and belonging" to develop the "whole child." *Achieving excellence* made inclusion and identity central to attaining equity and excellence.

Educators in our districts developed innovative projects to promote aspects of these new policy directions. Working with our diverse team of graduate students, we undertook case studies of each of these districts and held twice-yearly retreats with them in Toronto. It was the educators' interests, not ours, that took us into new terrain that addressed student learning and engagement, well-being, and identity.

In addition to an online technical report and several peer-reviewed research articles, listed at the back of this book, the products of our work are now spread across four books—*Five Paths of Student Engagement, Well-Being in Schools, Leadership From the Middle,* and this final volume: *The Age of Identity.*[7]

This is how we came to the topic of identity. We followed the interests of the educators in the 10 districts. We didn't decide to study and then write a book about identity. In many ways, the *Age of Identity* wrote us!

We have brought to this book the evidence of this research along with occasional references to other projects in which we have subsequently been engaged, the intellectual traditions in which we have been trained, and our interpretations of key contemporary sources on identity. At times, we have included reflections on our own biographies and identities. We have used all this to contribute to the field of identity in education in a way that may vary from accounts by people who have researched the topic in a different way, at a different time, in a different place, or from a different standpoint.

We do not presume to offer a definitive work on identity, or to provide comprehensive coverage of any or all types of identity. But we hope other researchers, educators, and readers in general will find things of value here that will deepen and challenge their own thinking on identity in schools today and help us bring together our different perspectives to work for the good of all students.

The Identity Agenda

As this book goes to press, we find ourselves in an intriguing historical moment. On the one hand, identities are being oppressed and excluded everywhere simply because of where people were born, what they look like, and how people in power respond to that.

- Economic inequality and the poverty that results from it are at their highest levels since before World War II.[8] According to Oxfam International, during the COVID-19 pandemic, the richest 1% acquired almost twice the world's wealth as everyone else put together.[9]

- Despite the *Black Lives Matter* movement, violence against and victimization of Black and Brown people continue to be inflicted by law enforcement officers on minority communities in many countries.[10]

- A 2023 survey in England of students' feelings about their safety in school found that less than half of those with "a gender identity other than male or female" or of those who were gay or bisexual felt safe compared with approximately three quarters of heterosexual students.[11]

- In Australia, the United States, and the United Kingdom, children who find themselves to be refugees, for no other reason than the geography of their birth, are sent to live in camps in conditions of squalor deliberately designed to deter other refugees.[12]

- In the United States, the only country that has refused to sign the 1989 *United Nations Convention on the Rights of the Child*, minors are imprisoned with adult felons.[13] More than a dozen U.S. states still shackle some pregnant women prisoners to their beds, in spite of protests by the American Medical Association.[14]

- In Canada, communities have been exhuming the remains of maltreated Indigenous children from residential schools that forcibly separated them from their language, families, and communities until as late as the mid-1990s.[15]

- The Russian war against Ukraine is attempting to erase national and cultural identity by, among even more cruel methods, forcing teachers in occupied territories to communicate in Russian and to remove Ukrainian cultural content from the curriculum.[16]

- Climate change, and the resistance of the traditional energy industry to combatting it, is posing the greatest and ultimate threat of all to the identities of the world's rising generations: extinction.[17]

On the other hand, in response to all this, groups who want to protect their privileges are twisting and turning aspects of these very real forms of social exclusion into full-scale culture wars. This is an *Alice in Wonderland* world of identity politics—of excessive focus on and moral panics about a tiny number of hot-button issues involving a few controversial textbooks and novels, statues and plaques, or bathrooms and pronouns.[18] The purpose of these fomented moral panics is to stoke up culture wars and inflame *identity politics* on a few symbolic issues to fill up the media bandwidth. This diverts people's anger and indignation away from massive economic and racial oppressions that have devastating consequences for monumental numbers of people with marginalized identities.

The expression *identity politics* goes back to a group known as the Combahee River Collective.[19] The Collective was a Black, feminist, lesbian organization in the 1970s, which felt that much of the feminist movement was racist and that parts of the civil rights movement were sexist and homophobic. It was an early example of what is now known

Groups who want to protect their privileges are twisting and turning aspects of these very real forms of social exclusion into full-scale culture wars.

as *intersectionality*. In a famous statement it made in 1977, the group introduced the term *identity politics* to help articulate its own feelings of oppression. Since then, like the term *woke* that has similar origins, *identity politics* has often been turned into a term of abuse by opponents of equity and inclusion.

This is a shame and an outrage. Identity politics are about the real differences that make many students prone to being marginalized and oppressed. They are a gateway into inclusion because they pinpoint who needs particular attention and why, as well as how the whole school culture needs to shift to make these accommodations possible. The point of identity politics should not be to put us into categories that set us against one another. It should be to include all of us, and bring us all together.

Historically, identity is a relatively recent phenomenon. In *Identity: Contemporary Identity Politics and the Struggle for Recognition*, Stanford University professor Francis Fukuyama argues that traditional societies had no need for any concept of identity or even of the self.[20] In agrarian societies, there were few differences other than biologically ascribed ones of age or gender.

> Social roles are both limited and fixed: a strict hierarchy
> is based on age and gender; everyone has the same
> occupation; one's entire life is in the same small village
> with a limited circle of friends and neighbors; one's
> religion and beliefs are shared by all; and social mobility is
> virtually impossible.[21]

There was no pluralism, movement, or choice—no need for anyone to distinguish themselves from anyone else. The world was what it was, and you were what you were. There wasn't much more to it.

With modernization, though, people took on new jobs, moved to cities, and met other kinds of people. Trade expanded, imperial colonization took place, mass migrations across continents and oceans occurred, and the printing press spread new ideas. Elites started to have leisure, time for reflection arose, travel and tourism evolved, women eventually took control of their own reproductive choices, and other life opportunities arose for them. Ideas of dignity and democracy took root, and oppressed and marginalized groups started to rebel and assert their rights. Television and then the internet spread images of how to look and to be, and medical science made it possible to hide the signs of aging, treat physical disabilities, and eventually enable people to affirm their gender identities.

In a couple of hundred years, a great deal happened. Now new identities are asserted, defended, and transformed all the time. The *Age of Identity* is not about finding or revealing our identities. It's about creating them anew.

The sense of liberation that comes with near-limitless choices, however, is coupled with feelings of what British social theorist Anthony Giddens calls "radical doubt."[22] "Modernity actually undermines the certainty of knowledge," Giddens writes.[23] As a result, we find that we no longer have confidence or clarity about who we really are.

Catalan sociologist Manuel Castells is more metaphorical. When traditional authority has collapsed, he says, "The king and the queen, the state and civil society, are both naked, and their children-citizens are wandering around a variety of foster homes."[24] However, Castells also points to new social movements of those who have experienced discrimination and who struggle for inclusion—women, people of color, disabled groups, and the LGBTQ+ community among them. These groups form the backbone of contemporary *identity politics.*

IDENTITY IS . . .

A universal part of modern human and educational development.

An integral element of adolescence and growing up.

An essential aspect of equity and inclusion.

A process, a quest, and a struggle.

Formed through relationships with others.

Something to acknowledge, represent, and celebrate.

Something that must sometimes be critiqued and challenged.

Multiple, complicated, and intersecting.

Presented differently to different groups and audiences.

Sometimes fluid, but never boundless.

Inseparable from who has the power to define it.

Often attacked, stigmatized, and suppressed.

Sometimes invisible, overlooked, and ignored.

An expression of personal uniqueness.

A resource for collective belonging.

LOOKING AHEAD

In this book we look at how education is affected by and in turn actively forms our identities and senses of ourselves. Identity is who we are. Including and engaging with diverse identities is essential to equity and achievement. Throughout this book, we will touch on all 15 statements and ideas about identity listed on the previous page.

We are living in a time when identity is all the rage—literally as well as figuratively. Hopefully, our research, and its illuminating examples, will help educators, parents, policy makers, and school board members move beyond rage to reconciliation. In the final chapter, we provide principles, protocols, and strategies to help people engage with diverse identities while also creating an educational and social world where we can all learn to live together to advance the common good.

Notes

1. Arendt, H. (2006). *Between past and future.* Penguin. (Original work published 1954)
2. Traub, G. W. (Ed.). (2008). *A Jesuit education reader.* Loyola.
3. Herdt, J. A. (2019). *Forming humanity: Reclaiming the German* Bildung *tradition.* University of Chicago Press.
4. Gay, G. (2018). *Culturally responsive teaching: Theory, research, and practice.* Teachers College Press.
5. Hargreaves, A., Shirley, D., Wangia, S., Bacon, C. K., & D'Angelo, M. (2018). *Leading from the middle: Spreading learning, well-being, and identity across Ontario.* Council of Ontario Directors of Education.
6. Hargreaves, A., & Shirley, D. (2022). *Well-being in schools: Three forces that will uplift your students in a volatile world.* ASCD; Shirley, D., & Hargreaves, A. (2021). *Five paths of student engagement: Blazing the trail to learning and success.* Solution Tree.
7. Ibid.; Hargreaves, A. (2023). *Leadership from the middle: The beating heart of educational transformation.* Routledge.
8. Coy, P. (2022, February 2). Wealth inequality is the highest since World War II. *The New York Times.* https://www.nytimes.com/2022/02/02/opinion/inequality-wealth-pandemic.html
9. Walker, J., Martin, M., Seery, E., Abdo, N., Kamande, A., & Lawson, M. (2022). *The commitment to reducing inequality index 2022.* Oxfam.
10. Jenkins, J., Mathur, M., Muyskens, J., Naklawahi, R., Rich, S., & Tran, A. B. (2023, March 29). Fatal force. *The Washington Post.* https://www.washingtonpost.com/graphics/investigations/police-shootings-database/
11. Weale, S. (2023, January 19). One in 10 pupils in England have missed school because they felt unsafe—survey. *The Guardian.* https://www.theguardian

.com/education/2023/jan/19/one-in-10-pupils-in-england-have-missed-school-because-they-felt-unsafe-survey

12. Andersson, H., & Laurent, A. (2021, May 24). *Children tell of neglect, filth, and fear in US asylum camps.* BBC. https://www.bbc.com/news/world-us-canada-57149721; Barnes, J. (2022). Suffering to save lives: Torture, cruelty, and moral disengagement in Australia's offshore detention centres. *Journal of Refugee Studies, 35*(4), 1508–1529; Connelly, A. (2021, February 22). Britain doesn't have a refugee crisis, so it invented one. *Foreign Policy.* https://foreignpolicy.com/2021/02/22/britain-refugee-crisis-europe-boris-johnson-priti-patel-asylum-seekers/

13. Equal Justice Initiative. (2017). *All children are children: Challenging abusive treatment of juveniles.* https://eji.org/wp-content/uploads/2019/10/AllChildrenAreChildren-2017-sm2.pdf

14. Hernandez, J. (2022, April 22). *More states are restricting the shackling of pregnant inmates, but it still occurs.* NPR. https://www.npr.org/2022/04/22/1093836514/shackle-pregnant-inmates-tennessee

15. Mosby, I. (2021, August 1). Canada's residential schools were a horror. *Scientific American.* https://www.scientificamerican.com/article/canadas-residential-schools-were-a-horror/

16. Walker, S., & Sauer, P. (2022, September 18). "No way I could work for the Russians": The Ukrainian teachers resisting occupation. *The Guardian.* https://www.theguardian.com/world/2022/sep/18/ukrainian-teachers-resist-russian-takeover-schools

17. Kaplan, A. (2023, March 20). World is on brink of catastrophic warming, UN climate change report says. *The Washington Post.* https://www.washingtonpost.com/climate-environment/2023/03/20/climate-change-ipcc-report-15/

18. For one example, see Yang, M. (2023, April 19). Florida board approves expansion of "don't say gay" ban to all school grades. *The Guardian.* https://www.theguardian.com/us-news/2023/apr/19/florida-education-board-approves-expansion-dont-say-gay-bill

19. Combahee River Collective. (1982). A Black feminist statement. In G. T. Hull, P. B. Scott, & B. Smith (Eds.), *But some of us are brave* (pp. 13–22). Feminist Press.

20. Fukuyama, F. (2019). *Identity: Contemporary identity politics and the struggle for recognition.* Farrar, Straus, & Giroux.

21. Ibid., p. 35.

22. Giddens, A. (1991). *Modernity and self-identity: Self and society in the late modern age.* Stanford University Press, p. 3.

23. Ibid., p. 21.

24. Castells, M. (1997). *The information age: Economy, society, and culture: Vol. 2. The power of identity.* Blackwell, p. 355.

About the Authors

Dennis Shirley is Gabelli Faculty Fellow and Professor of Formative Education at the Lynch School of Education and Human Development at Boston College. He has led and advised many educational change initiatives. He was the principal investigator of the Massachusetts Coalition for Teacher Quality and Student Achievement, a federally funded improvement network that united 18 urban schools, 7 higher education institutions, and 16 community-based organizations. He has conducted in-depth studies on school innovations in England, Germany, Canada, and South Korea. Dennis has been a visiting professor at Harvard University in the United States, at Venice International University in Italy, at the National Institute of Education in Singapore, at the University of Barcelona in Spain, and at the University of Stavanger in Norway. He is a Richard von Weizsäcker Fellow at the Robert Bosch Academy in Berlin, Germany. Dennis holds a doctorate in education from Harvard University.

Andy Hargreaves is a research professor at Boston College and a visiting professor at the University of Ottawa. He is an elected member of the U.S. National Academy of Education. He is past president of the International Congress for School Effectiveness and Improvement, adviser in education to the first minister of Scotland, and former adviser to the premier of Ontario. Andy is cofounder and president of the ARC Education Project: a group of nations committed to humanistic goals in education. Andy's more than 30 books have attracted 8 Outstanding Writing Awards. He has been honored for services to public education and educational research in the United States, the United Kingdom, and Canada. Andy is ranked by *Education Week* among the top 20 scholars with most influence on U.S. education policy debate. In 2015, Boston College gave him its Excellence in Teaching With Technology Award. Andy's most recent book is *Leadership From the Middle: The Beating Heart of Educational Transformation.*

The Age of Identity is the fifth book that Dennis and Andy have written together.

CHAPTER 1

To Be, Or Not to Be

No man is an island entire of itself; every man is a piece
of the continent, a part of the main.

—John Donne (1624)

The question of
identity is not just
about *them*, the
others. Identity
issues affect all
of us.

Who Do We Think We Are?

Who do you think you are? It's a simple enough question. It should have an obvious answer. Increasingly, though, knowing and saying who we are is getting more and more complicated.

> *Which cultures should be celebrated?*
>
> *Whose historical accomplishments should be honored?*
>
> *What pronouns should we use for ourselves and others?*
>
> *How do we talk about children with learning disabilities?*
>
> *Are all of us neurodiverse?*
>
> *What signs do we put on the bathroom door?*
>
> *Which identities should be included in the curriculum, and which ones left out?*
>
> *Who will decide?*
>
> *And who do we think are the kids in our homes and our schools?*
>
> *Do we truly know our kids?*
>
> *How do we get past the impressions our kids present to us?*

Identity has become one of the most controversial issues of our time. Potential school board members run for election with platforms that articulate provocative views about identity. School administrators get fired for saying the wrong thing in relation to identity. Statues are raised or removed because of it. The curriculum is constantly changing in response to it. The signs of the *Age of Identity* are everywhere. They are impossible to ignore. But it's often difficult to know what to do.

The question of identity is not just about *them*, the others—people who are different and who have been excluded or oppressed in one way or another. Identity issues affect all of us. It's hard to know *how* to be unless we know *who* we are. It's also difficult to know *who* we are unless we know *what* we are and are *not* a part of.

Human beings are not feral creatures. We do not grow up among wild beasts, or alone, all by ourselves. Maintaining a clear sense of who we are becomes very difficult if we get stranded on a desert island or are condemned to solitary confinement in prison. This is why isolation is a basic method of interrogation.

> Identity issues affect all of us. It's hard to know *how* to be unless we know *who* we are. It's also difficult to know *who* we are unless we know *what* we are and are *not* a part of.

To feel alone, abandoned, and without any sense of belonging to anything is one of the worst conditions we can imagine. "No man is an island entire of itself; every man is a piece of the continent, a part of the main," wrote the 17th century English poet John Donne.[1] Tom Hanks, in the movie *Cast Away*, needed his imaginary friend, Wilson, a volleyball, in order to survive.[2] This is why former U.K. prime minister Margaret Thatcher was factually as well as morally wrong when she declared, "There is no such thing as society. There are individual men and women and there are families."[3]

Educators play an important role in helping students deal with identity issues. From the moment children start school, teachers are already helping them learn about their identities and how they can and should be developed.

Identity matters for everyone. Recall your first date and how anxious (and excited) you were about how you would come across to your new romantic interest. Did you suddenly feel differently about yourself when you became a parent or a grandparent for the first time? What if you moved to another country as an adult or a child? Did you worry whether people would accept you, what your accent was like, and if you would fit in? If you went to live away from home at university or college, did you suddenly feel different, more independent, and free?

Some changes in identity can be abrupt, unexpected, traumatic, or revelatory. They can make us question, redefine, or reembrace the very essence of who we or other people are.

Korean-born, U.S.-adopted identical twin sisters Emily Bushnell and Molly Sinert, competitors on CBS TV's *Amazing Race*, had only recently discovered each other. During their mid-30s, an at-home DNA test revealed to each twin the existence of the other twin. When they met for the first time, Bushnell said, "We talked a lot. We cried. We laughed. We got a chance to be sisters together."[4] Discovering in midlife that they had a twin and were a twin was transformative to their sense of identity.

Americans regularly celebrate Rosa Parks, whose refusal to go to the back of the bus with other Black Americans in Alabama sparked the civil rights movement in 1955. Yet most are unaware that Parks also attached significance to her identity as the descendant of her white great-grandfather, James Percival. He was an unfree, indentured immigrant laborer from Glasgow in the United Kingdom. Percival married Parks's "unmixed" mother in 1860, when she was still enslaved at a plantation outside of Montgomery, Alabama.[5]

Irene is one of nine intersex persons who were interviewed for *Teen Vogue* magazine in 2019. She was 22 when she discovered she was intersex after watching a video on the topic and then tracing her medical records. "Discovering the truth was the best thing that ever happened to me," she said. "I wish I knew the truth from the start. I could've avoided years of pain, shame, and self-hatred."[6] In the words of another interviewee, Danielle from Germany, "embracing my intersex identity gave me a truly worthy purpose that consistently grounds me and sets me in the right direction."[7] Interestingly, one of the seven items on the menu at TeenVogue.com, alongside others like style, politics, culture, and shopping, is identity.

Revelations like these are the essence of the U.K. celebrity genealogical TV series *Who Do You Think You Are?* and its U.S. equivalent, *Finding Your Roots*. Singer-songwriter Carly Simon, for example, had always been told by her Cuban-born grandmother that she was descended from the king of Spain, but this turned out to be a cover story. DNA testing revealed that her grandmother was 40% Black. Simon's great-grandmother, it turned out, was 100% Black. As *Finding Your Roots* host Henry Louis Gates Jr. commented, "We have never tested a white person as Black as you."[8] Simon found this to be "completely fascinating."[9]

But these racial revelations don't always yield the same result. When confronted on Trisha Goddard's U.K. TV show with DNA evidence that he was 14% Sub-Saharan African, American white supremacist Paul Craig Cobb dismissed the evidence as "statistical noise."[10] This echoed the tendency of many other white supremacists faced with similar evidence to reject it as flawed science, to invoke conspiracy theories, or to recalculate what whiteness means. Identity shocks can open people up—or just make them deepen their denial.

Who Do They Think They Are?

When children or adults have crossed us or betrayed us, or let themselves down, asking them who on earth they think they are is a criticism and a challenge.

When a model student bullies a classmate, when a star sports performer rubs their victory in the face of their opponents, or if our own partner has an affair with someone else, we often hurl this outraged question at them: "Who *on earth* do *you* think you are?" Transgressions like these raise questions about whether the student, the sports star, or our partner has betrayed their own identity, or revealed themselves to be someone else altogether.

This happens when people we know, love, or respect fall from grace—when their immense accomplishments are negated by discoveries that they have gone to prison for swindling their associates, have been distributing child sex abuse material, have blurted out racial insults, or have sexually harassed a colleague. What became of them? Did they turn into someone else? Did we never really know them in the first place? Indeed, do we ever, fully, know anybody at all, including ourselves? People may not be all that they seem. Like a ship using a false flag to deceive its enemy, they may have been hiding their true colors all along.

Conversely, educators know all too well the phenomenon of young people being or becoming far more than they have always seemed. The struggling student who becomes a late bloomer, the shy classmate who turns into a star on stage, the dour plodder who becomes a creative genius once their teacher finds and ignites their passion—these kinds of transformations are what teachers live for. Sometimes, teachers and parents seem to know their children even better than the children know themselves!

Learning How Not to Be

Identity matters for all of us. Who we are, what we will become, and how we develop character, become citizens, experience belonging, and learn to be inclusive of others who are different from us—these purposes of education and schools are fundamental. They also have a long and distinguished pedigree.

In Greek philosophy, Aristotle said that education should lead toward habitual ways of thinking and acting that promote four cardinal virtues: prudence, justice, temperance, and fortitude.[11] Friedrich Froebel, the inventor of the kindergarten, disagreed with the harsh discipline he saw in German education in the 19th century and created a gentler way of teaching that recognized the child's need for play, dance, art, and nature study.[12] Early childhood legend Maria Montessori took Froebel's ideas one step further and asked educators to refrain from the imposition of a preestablished curriculum in order to follow "the natural physiological and psychological development of the child."[13] She designed learning so that children could freely circulate among play centers to learn topics of their own choosing at their own pace. Likewise, American progressive educator John Dewey advised teachers that work should not be drudgery, nor should play be mere amusement, aimlessness, or relief from work. Rather, like botany and outdoor gardening, work and play should be integrated parts of young people's learning and development.[14]

For all these visionary educators, the growing child was a whole person requiring careful guidance in the development of their complete identities over years of maturation and growth.

But for several decades that spanned the turn of this century, identity issues dropped to the bottom of the list of many school systems' priorities. In some cases, the most zealous reformers struck them off the page completely. Still, the question of identity never went away entirely. It just went underground.

In the most famous soliloquy ever written, Shakespeare's Hamlet asks:

> *To be, or not to be: that is the question:*
> *Whether 'tis nobler in the mind to suffer*
> *The slings and arrows of outrageous fortune,*
> *Or to take arms against a sea of troubles,*
> *And by opposing end them.*[15]

Hamlet is pondering whether life, given all its "slings and arrows," is worth living at all. But "to be, or not to be," could also be about *how* we live, not just whether we live or die. Should we live fully and completely, or barely exist?

For 40 years, many of the world's educational systems, and the international metrics that compared their performances, operated as if they were teaching young people how and who *not* to be. Literacy, mathematics, and science crowded out disciplines like history, music, and the visual arts. Measurable results focused on achievement targets, testing, attendance, performance, high school completion, and graduation rates.

Educators found themselves driven by an agenda emphasizing student achievement and effort. They devoted little or no attention to engagement, well-being, or identity. Schooling was about what students did and how they performed, not who they were or what they might become.

An inspired but ultimately unsuccessful attempt to turn back this tide toward developing young people as human beings in their emotional, moral, and spiritual lives, rather than focusing only on their cognitive knowledge and skills, was attempted by the United Nations Educational, Scientific, and Cultural Organization in 1996. At that time an "International Commission on Education for the Twenty-First Century" composed of representatives from 15 countries issued a report called *Learning: The Treasure Within.*[16] It proposed four pillars for the future of education. Two of them were about *learning to know* and *learning to do.*

 Learning to know defines the traditional goal to help students acquire "broad general education with the possibility of in-depth work on a selected number of subjects."[17]

 Learning to do is to acquire "a competence that enables people to deal with a variety of situations" and teams in order to "try out and develop their abilities by becoming involved in work development schemes."[18]

The problem, the International Commission warned, was that the offerings of schools were too narrow. "Formal education focused mainly, if not exclusively, on *learning to know*, and to a lesser extent on *learning to do.*"[19]

Nonetheless, in spite of these warnings, many of the world's education systems, especially the Anglo American group of nations, alongside transnational organizations such as the World Bank and the Organisation for Economic Co-operation and Development, pressed on with driving up results in literacy, mathematics, and science. Usually this was at the expense of other areas of learning and development. Students' social and emotional learning and learning outdoors, in nature, were pushed to the margins. *Learning to know* eclipsed everything else.

During this period, student identity was irrelevant in most educational policies. The nearest thing to it was a demographic or legal category. Schools classified students by labels such as *African American, immigrant, English learner,* or *child with identified special needs.* This was perhaps well intended, but also often misleading and bemusing. Brazilian immigrants to the United States, for example, have no category that applies to them. And more and more people now, like Andy's five grandchildren, are mixed heritage and don't fit any single box at all.

Educators might celebrate Black History Month, Cinco de Mayo, or Lunar New Year, but in terms of official policies, these recognitions of cultural diversity have been peripheral to making achievement gains or improving high school graduation rates. The content of the curriculum

---

Icon source: Gatot supandri/istock.com

and how it did or didn't mesh with young people's cultures and identities was officially unimportant. Who students were and what they felt they were part of was tangential to the drive for higher performance and better delivery.

Learning to Live Together

So, as well as *learning to know* and *learning to do*, what else should our young people be learning? What were the missing pillars? They were existential and social. They were about *learning to be* and *learning to live together*.

Learning to be means giving every child and adolescent "every possible opportunity" to develop their personality and be able to act with ever greater "freedom of thought, judgment, feeling and imagination."[20] "None of the talents which are hidden like buried treasure in every person must be left untapped."[21]

Learning to live together involves creating "a spirit of tolerance and dialogue" among the young.[22] This must be done "so that the legitimate aspiration to preserve traditions and a collective identity is never seen as incompatible with a spirit of fellowship and solidarity, and so that the maintenance of social cohesion never implies a closer, inward-looking attitude or fundamentalism."[23]

The International Commission was named after its chair, Jacques Delors, the eighth president of the European Commission. Delors cared about peace, unity, and belonging. For him, *learning to live together* was the most important pillar of all. Alarmed by the inability of nations and the United Nations to stop international conflicts, his commission asked: Who should we become, so that we can live together? How should we promote the identities of all young people, so they can lead their lives with inclusion and a sense of belonging?

The message was crystal clear: It's no longer enough to know how to memorize content or make things. We must also, and perhaps especially, *learn to be* and *learn to live together*.

Icon Source: Gatot supandri/istock.com

Identity and Inclusion

Historically, a lot of the work on identity, particularly on adolescent identity, has focused on helping all young people to become their best selves when they are separating from their parents and forging their own personalities. This remains an essential part of the *Age of Identity*. In recent years, though, identity issues have become both more dominant and more disputed. Six reasons for this are set out in Figure 1.1.

Figure 1.1	Social Causes of the Rising Interest in Identity	
	Generational	Generation X (born 1965–1980) is independent and calculative about work–life balance. Millennials (1981–1996) focus on developing their own personalities. In each case, the individual is at the center of how the generation understands itself.[24]
	Technological	Expanded adolescent use of smartphones since 2012 has led to a preoccupation with image enhancement and with virtual identities designed to maximize followers and friends.[25]
	Psychological	Mounting social problems have been met with a proliferation of psychological coping strategies that turn people inward with practical recommendations promoting wellness, meditation, life coaching, self-help, and self-care.[26]
	Medical	Advances in medical technologies mean that biologically given characteristics of age, gender, or appearance can be altered through cosmetic procedures and gender affirmation.[27]
	Global	War, climate change, and poverty drive people to migrate elsewhere. This increases awareness of and resentment about cultural differences. National identity is called into question.[28]
	Cultural-Political	Increasing and unsolved economic inequalities are kept off the public agenda, and politics has organized instead around other lightning rod social issues such as transgender identities, textbook content, pronoun usage, and white privilege.[29]

Source: Generational, Psychological, Global icons by iStock.com/appleuzr; Cultural Political icon by iStock.com/Yuriy Altukhov

In addition to and arising out of these multiple forces has been a significant push in educational institutions and workplaces toward inclusion of different cultures and identities as ways to increase equity and opportunity. These moves, in turn, have been met with an indignant backlash from groups who have felt threatened or overlooked by these developments. Increased *inclusion*, on the one hand, has come up against *righteous indignation*, on the other.

Inclusion affects us all. Can you think of a time when, in a nontrivial way, you were, or you felt, excluded for one reason or another? Perhaps teenage peers looked down on you because they thought you were too much into your books. Maybe you stood out because you had a different accent, were the only child with a different skin color, or came from the "wrong" side of town.

Increased inclusion, on the one hand, has come up against righteous indignation, on the other.

Were you ever bullied, teased, or picked on? What did it feel like if you were making your career as a young woman in a workplace dominated by older men? Suppose you were gay or lesbian in a place where coming out could end your career?

Maybe you are a single parent whose social invitations dried up when you were no longer part of a couple. How have you felt if your own child has been mocked because of a stutter or another speech disorder? If you have hit your 60s, do you feel offended when waitstaff direct you to the worst tables at the back of restaurants?

Hopefully, the example you recalled, although painful or embarrassing, was a transient one. But what if you were to experience, or indeed already do experience, these sorts of exclusions every day? How degrading and dispiriting that must be.

Over 50 years of policies and legislation have attempted to bring about greater equity by tackling forms of exclusion that hold whole groups of people back because of prejudice and discrimination that has nothing to do with their performance. Equal pay for women, prohibition of racial and ethnic discrimination, rights of access and inclusivity for people with disabilities, outlawing of sexual harassment, LGBTQ+ rights in the workplace, and the legalization of same-sex marriage have made the most egregious forms of exclusion illegal in many societies.

In schools, inclusion policies first emerged as synonyms for special education provisions so that young people with physical or mental disabilities would not be excluded from the learning experiences and opportunities that others are able to enjoy. Inclusion here often meant putting an end to separate classes and schools for students with special needs. Or it involved halting the practice of withdrawing students periodically from their regular classes for additional support.

Over time, inclusion in some educational systems moved closer to the more all-encompassing understanding of inclusion and diversity in workplaces. This has meant that more schools now try to ensure that all students and staff have equal opportunities, are respected, and feel they belong.

In September 2022, the United Nations convened a "Transforming Education Summit" in New York City that placed "commitment to addressing educational exclusion" as its top priority.[30] The UN identified several identity groups experiencing social exclusion as "girls and young women; learners with disabilities; Indigenous populations, cultural and linguistic minorities; rural learners; stateless people; internally displaced peoples; [and] refugees."[31] It warned that without developing new strategies to "ensure the inclusion of all in the education system," the world's countries would fail to meet its sustainable development goals—especially the goal of providing "quality education for all," regardless of one's background or ascribed identity.[32]

In addition to our collaborative work with educators in Ontario, Andy has codirected with Professor Jess Whitley a developmental evaluation of the implementation of the inclusion strategy of another Canadian province: Nova Scotia. Both systems have adopted an especially bold approach to inclusion. For example, Nova Scotia's Inclusive Education Policy states that

> inclusive education is a commitment to ensuring a high-quality, culturally and linguistically responsive and equitable education to support the well-being and achievement of every student. All students should feel that they belong in an inclusive school—accepted, safe, and valued—so they can best learn and succeed.[33]

As in Ontario, the groups specifically served and supported by Nova Scotia's Inclusive Education Policy extend beyond those with identified special educational needs. Inclusion is the path to equity for all students. The strategy is especially meant to support "success for students who are historically marginalized and racialized (African Nova Scotian and Mi'kmaw students) or who come from other groups that have been traditionally under-represented and under-served, including, but not limited to, students with special needs and those struggling with poverty."[34] In these respects, inclusion and identity are intertwined.

Identity and Indignation

The *Age of Identity* has emerged and advanced out of these kinds of movements for equity and inclusion. But they have not gone unopposed. Struggles over identity and recognition now span a spectrum from broad arguments about the importance of inclusion with which almost everyone might agree, to disputes about the relative worth of different identities that some groups want to cherish, and others say should be canceled. Sometimes, in these back-and-forth debates between race and social class, between religious freedom and human rights, and about what the proper definition of a woman is, it can feel impossible to find common ground.

Twenty-five U.S. states have passed legislation prescribing and proscribing how and whether teachers should address issues of race and gender identity.[35] *The Washington Post* reports that 64 bills are being enforced that curtail teachers' freedom to discuss these topics.[36] In the most severe instances, parents can lodge complaints against teachers and school librarians online that can result in disciplinary measures and terminated employment.[37]

In England, the government insists that children should learn an airbrushed version of history that downplays the negative aspects of an empire that once covered a quarter of the globe.[38] After the invasion of Ukraine in 2022, Russia burned textbooks and passed new laws to inscribe Russian identity in the curriculum, while Ukraine reciprocated by removing many elements of Russian language and literature from its curriculum.[39] In May 2022, a wave of protests broke out in India after a new curriculum promoted Hindu nationalism and omitted the contributions of the country's minority Muslim population.[40]

Canada too is witnessing rising indignation about identity issues in schools. Ontario's Waterloo school district, with a long-standing German and Mennonite heritage, has seen recent settlement from Arabic and Punjabi speakers.[41] The district's Muslim director also claims Indigenous Polynesian ancestry. Heated discussions in school board meetings have included concerns about two books that discuss asexuality and transgender identities, and about the director's advice to parents to avoid Halloween costume day, decorations, and treats in school. Threats to the director and school board members were traced to local phone numbers but also to area codes as far away as Texas.

Not all disputes and debates about identity issues can be indisputably categorized as good and bad or right and wrong. Consider these questions concerning gender (see boxed text).

QUESTIONS ON GENDER

- How often should educators make sure that girls (and boys) study topics and read about protagonists that are girl-friendly or girl-powered?

- Is the elevation of female protagonists as prominent figures of strength and power in children's literature and movies an unambiguously positive move toward gender equity, or does it also contribute to a decline in positive role models for boys whose relative achievement levels have been sinking?

- Should Black boys more often be taught by Black males who can be role models for them, rather than by white female teachers, no matter how empathetic those teachers might be?

- How can Nordic countries, with outstanding records of gender equity, be fully inclusive of newly immigrant cultures that do not make gender equity a priority, and may even be opposed to it?

What should we do about aspects of multiple identity that are conflicting and contradictory? What about marginalized religious groups that oppress gender-based minorities? Or impoverished white working-class communities that also contain strains of racism and xenophobia? What about people with identities that are culturally marginalized or oppressed, but who also possess immense wealth privilege?

Meghan Markle, wife of the United Kingdom's Prince Harry, and Rishi Sunak, the country's prime minister, are both people of color. They have been subject to egregious racial abuse from members of the British establishment. Yet, as people who married into two of the wealthiest families in the world, can their experiences of oppression be equated with or elevated above those of a poor Black hospital cleaner or a white homeless person, for example?

What do we do when people are oppressed or marginalized in some respects, but are oppressors or privileged in others? Do we try to weigh the scales and say that sometimes the good counterbalances the evil? Do we insist that any evil, however unintended or culturally widespread at the time, cancels out all the other good that a person may have done?

Or do we avoid identity controversies altogether, hoping that they will all go away, and that we will just be able to get back to familiar territory, like "the basics"?

Sometimes, there just isn't one incontrovertible answer. For instance, we should certainly dismantle or critically recast the colonial statues of owners and traders of enslaved people. But do racist slurs against Native Americans by John Muir, founder of the Sierra Club, which were common in his time, invalidate his foundational contribution to the environmental movement? Should former U.S. president Bill Clinton, feminist author Naomi Wolf, singer-songwriter Kris Kristofferson, gay U.S. presidential candidate Pete Buttigieg, and former Ontario socialist premier Bob Rae all rescind and repay their prestigious Rhodes Scholarship awards now that Cecil Rhodes, for whom they were named and by whose will they were founded, has been exposed as the architect of South African apartheid?

There are no easy answers to such probing questions. We must be able to reason our way through them in a respectful and empathetic way. There should be room for dissident perspectives to be aired, even (and especially) when we emphatically disagree with them.

Identity issues are a tangled web. The rest of this book weaves its way through this knotted social fabric of identity. In the closing chapter, it concludes with ideas, strategies, and protocols about how to do that together.

Identity has become too much of a tinderbox of politicized emotion. We've all experienced how an anachronistic term or a misplaced pronoun can ignite a firestorm of anger. It is too easy to assume the role of Grand Inquisitor who takes it upon themselves to go about denouncing the supposedly less enlightened. It's time to get beyond all of that. It's time to push hard to determine what most of us can agree on together, and to establish ways of living with and engaging in dialogue together about those aspects of identity on which we initially differ. The place to begin is with our kids, in our schools.

Collective Identity

The schools that we studied were built on the belief that what is *essential for some* children is *good for all* of them. For example, technological enhancements of learning for students with disabilities are beneficial for other learners, too. Gender-neutral toilets can be designed in ways that mean better bathrooms for all students. Indigenous ways of knowing that connect learning to the outdoors, and that forge spiritual connections to something greater than our individual senses of self, can be inspiring and engaging for young people from all cultures and

> Identity has become too much of a tinderbox of politicized emotion.

> What is *essential for some* children is *good for all* of them.

communities. In the hands of talented educators and supportive communities, the identities of a particular group can contribute ideas and practices that benefit everyone.

This is one way to approach an important theme of our book: moving toward some sense of *collective identity*. What things can we empathize with and agree on even though we may differ on other issues? Are there some things greater than all of us we can commit to without these being imperial, Western, or predominantly male, for instance?

The bulwarks of society that people relied upon for generations to give their lives structure and value, like conventional religion, traditional families, and stable political states, have been eroded and sometimes completely lost. Commonality is not so obviously achievable anymore.

Collective identities needn't mean *common* or *imposed* identities. The point is not to make identities identical. But they must amount to more than mere collections or aggregates. There must be boundaries and borders, somewhere. And we must discuss and debate these without prejudging the outcomes. What are sustainable immigration strategies that will enable a host country to grow and change by engaging with new identities without the country losing all its existing historic and cultural identity? Conversely, what immigration rates and levels will provide enough new taxpayers to sustain an aging host population? What does neuroscience tell us about the appropriate age of human brain development and maturity that should inform when young people are allowed and entitled to make medically irreversible decisions about their gender identity? What racial or homophobic comments must be treated as unacceptable even if they are made by someone who is economically oppressed, has mental health problems, or feels protected by their privilege or their religion?

What will become of us? How can we decide? Can we create a sense of belonging and inclusion in which all students can truly flourish? In practical terms, what must be done so that all students feel welcomed as whole people in our schools?

What about working-class students who see little or no discussion of labor history, craft pride, or collective class solidarity in their schools? We must learn to work with people who are different from us as well as those who are the same. Our world should not just be about "me and my group," but about all our groups together—except for the most heinous.

Consider an example. We spent seven years working with educators in five states in the Pacific Northwest of the United States to increase student engagement in rural schools. Many of the educators there, like a lot of other U.S. educators, were (unlike us) supporters of the presidential candidate at the time, Donald Trump. One of them was a

Collective identities needn't mean common or imposed identities. The point is not to make identities identical. But they must amount to more than mere collections or aggregates.

Teacher of the Year finalist for his state. He was awesome at engaging his students—the purpose of our project. He was also a strong pro-life advocate—a position that neither of us hold. Yet he and his wife had fostered a great many children and teenagers with severe physical and mental disabilities as acts of immense care and sacrifice. In our work with him and his many colleagues, we concentrated on what we held in common that would benefit the children they taught, not on other things that divided us.

This is the *Age of Identity* we address in this book. It is rooted in our work with Ontario's educators while drawing on our other firsthand research. It also builds on classic and contemporary literature on identity and identity politics to forge a new way forward in our classrooms, among our colleagues, and with our communities that can create educational experiences that are inclusive of all but the most hateful identities. Identity should be a key to inclusion, not a lock that shuts people out. With greater inclusion, we will often get greater equity and increased belonging. Given where our troubled world is right now, there are few better things we could commit to than that.

The Flow of the Book

Identity should be a key to inclusion, not a lock that shuts people out.

The book is organized into seven chapters. Chapter 2 looks at self and identity development. It examines classic theories of how selves develop across the life span, through a complex interaction between individual development and socialization, from childhood into adolescence, and through many phases of adulthood.

Chapter 3 points to how our identities are not only inside us, like objects or things, but also emerge through our everyday interactions with other people, especially in relation to family, friends, and teachers who are significant for us.

Chapter 4 discusses how to celebrate and include identities, and how to grant them greater recognition and bring them to the fore in how we think about young people's development.

Chapter 5 looks at how and in what ways identities are multiple and not singular. It examines what happens when people have combinations of different identities in terms of nationality, social class, and race.

Chapter 6 engages with and further develops one of the most topical and controversial ways of thinking about multiple identities: the concept of *intersectional* forms of marginalization. This captures how many people experience multiple, compounded, and sometimes contradictory relationships to oppression in their lives and their education.

The final chapter, Chapter 7, asks what leaders of all kinds can do to work through and with the *Age of Identity* to create the best possible inclusive and equitable schools and school systems where all students of every class, color, creed, and other forms of identity can flourish and be successful.

BE A BUFFALO

A storm has come upon us. It's been brewing for some time. Culture wars. Identity politics. Parents who are against kids being exposed to controversial and inappropriate material. Teachers and administrators who feel constantly under attack. Parents' rights. Teachers' plights. There is hostility, anxiety, panic, and fear. Should you shelter from the storm? Should you try to outrun it? The storm's not going away, though. What should you do?

Out on the plains, where the buffalo roam, animals can sense when storm clouds are gathering. Some hide. Others flee. They try to keep ahead of the howling wind and the lashing rain. But the storm catches up with them. Soon, they find they are running with the storm and in it. The storm is all around them, all the time. They are trapped. It's exhausting.

The buffalo sense the storm is coming too. But they adopt a different strategy from the other animals. They turn around to face the storm. It seems a reckless thing to do. Yet it makes complete sense. Turning into the storm is unpleasant, dangerous even. The threat and the fear abate quickly, though. By heading into the storm, the buffalo are also moving through it. Soon, they are out on the other side. The storm is behind them. The danger has passed.[42]

How will you deal with the identity storms that have come upon our schools, threatened our communities, and consumed our politics? Will you try to avoid the storms? Will you run and hide? Or will you be a buffalo and face the storms head-on, knowing that, on the other side, things can be better for everyone?

When we are confronting the threats of climate change, pandemics, racism, violence, xenophobia, and war, there is so much to fight for in education without fighting unnecessarily against each other and among ourselves. How can we learn to be? How can we learn to live together? These are the questions.

Notes

1. Donne, J. (1999). *Devotions upon emergent occasions and death's duel.* Random House, p. 17. (Original work published 1623)

2. Starkey, S., Hanks, T., Zemeckis, R., Rapke, J. (Producers), & Zemeckis, R. (Director). (2000). *Cast away* [Film]. 20th Century Fox.

3. BBC. (2013, April 8). *In quotes: Margaret Thatcher.* https://www.bbc.com/news/uk-politics-10377842

4. Ilgenfritz, R. (2022, October 6). Ardmore woman teams up with long-lost twin for "Amazing Race" journey: Emily Bushnell met her twin for the first time last year. *Main Line Times and Suburban.* https://www.mainlinemedianews.com/2022/10/06/ardmore-woman-teams-up-with-her-long-lost-twin-for-an-amazing-journey/

5. Parks, R., & Haskin, J. (1999). *Rosa Parks: My story.* Dial Books.

6. Lindahl, H. (2019, October 25). 9 young people on how they found out they are intersex. *Teen Vogue.* https://www.teenvogue.com/gallery/young-people-on-how-they-found-out-they-are-intersex

7. Ibid.

8. Gates, H. L., Jr. (2019, February 28). *Finding your roots season 4: Carly Simon clip* [Video]. YouTube. https://www.youtube.com/watch?v=EpLNkuVCp8g

9. Ibid.

10. Collins, L. (2013, November 11). Exclusive: Watch the moment white supremacist trying to take over North Dakota town refuses to fist bump Black host after she tells him he is 14 per cent African. *Daily Mail.* https://www.dailymail.co.uk/news/article-2493491/White-supremacist-Craig-Cobbs-DNA-test-reveals-hes-14-African.html

11. Aristotle. (1966). *The basic works of Aristotle.* Random House.

12. Wasmuth, H. (2020). *Fröbel's pedagogy of kindergarten and play.* Routledge.

13. Montessori, M. (1914). *Dr. Montessori's own handbook.* Schocken, p. 17.

14. Dewey, J. (1916). *Democracy and education.* Free Press, pp. 194–206.

15. Poetry Foundation. (2023). *Speech: "To be or not to be, that is the question" by William Shakespeare.* https://www.poetryfoundation.org/poems/56965/speech-to-be-or-not-to-be-that-is-the-question

16. International Commission on Education for the Twenty-First Century. (1996). *Learning: The treasure within.* UNESCO.

17. Ibid., p. 23.

18. Ibid.

19. Ibid., p. 86.

20. Ibid., pp. 94–95.

21. Ibid., p. 23.

22. Ibid., p. 212.

23. Ibid.

24. Twenge, J. M., & Campbell, W. K. (2009). *The narcissism epidemic.* Atria.

25. Eler, A. (2017). *The selfie generation: How our self-images are changing our notions of privacy, sex, consent, and culture.* Skyhorse.

26. McLaughlin, K. (2012). *Surviving identity: Vulnerability and the psychology of recognition.* Routledge; Moscowitz, E. S. (2001). *In therapy we trust: America's obsession with self-fulfillment.* Johns Hopkins.

27. Schechter, L. S. (2020). *Gender confirmation surgery: Principles and techniques for an emerging field.* Springer.

28. Bauman, Z. (2000). *Liquid modernity.* Polity.

29. Michaels, W. B. (2006). *The trouble with diversity: How we learned to love identity and ignore inequality.* Picador.

30. United Nations. (2023). *Transforming Education Summit convened by the United Nations secretary-general: Concept note and programme outline.* Author, p. 7.

31. Ibid., p. 53.

32. Ibid.

33. Province of Nova Scotia. (2019, August). *Inclusive education policy.* https://www.ednet.ns.ca/docs/inclusiveeducationpolicyen.pdf

34. Ibid.

35. Natanson, H. (2023, March 17). Few legal challenges to laws limiting lessons on race, gender. *The Washington Post.* https://www.washingtonpost.com/education/2023/03/17/legal-challenges-gender-critical-race-theory/

36. Natanson, H., Morse, C. E., Narayanswamy, A., & Brause, C. (2022, October 18). An explosion of culture war laws is changing schools. Here's how. *The Washington Post.* https://www.washingtonpost.com/education/2022/10/18/education-laws-culture-war/

37. Abdal-Baqui, O., & Calfas, J. (2022, January 26). New Virginia hotline lets parents report "divisive teaching practices." *The Wall Street Journal.* https://www.wsj.com/articles/new-virginia-hotline-lets-parents-report-divisive-teaching-practices-11643236044

38. Koram, K. (2023, April 4). Teaching the "benefits" of the British empire is just another attempt to stoke the culture war. *The Guardian.* https://www.theguardian.com/commentisfree/2022/apr/04/pupils-benefits-empire-ignorance-royals-caribbean-windrush

39. Roth, A. (2022, April 23). Lessons in patriotism used to justify Ukraine invasion to Russia's children. *The Guardian.* https://www.theguardian.com/world/2022/apr/23/lessons-in-patriotism-used-to-justify-ukraine-invasion-to-russias-children

40. Krishnan, M. (2022, May 25). Is the BJP changing textbooks to promote Hindu nationalism? *Deutsche Welle.* https://www.dw.com/en/india-is-the-bjp-altering-school-curriculum-to-promote-hindu-nationalism/a-61932435

41. Alphonso, C. (2022, October 14). Why a Waterloo, Ont., school board has emerged as a battleground for ideological politics. *The Globe and Mail.* https://www.theglobeandmail.com/canada/article-why-a-waterloo-ont-school-board-has-emerged-as-a-battleground-for/

42. Rinella, S. (2008). *American buffalo: In search of a lost icon.* Random House.

CHAPTER 2

The Developing Self

All I can do is be me—whoever that is.

—Bob Dylan (1965)

Developing
self-knowledge
is or should be a
prime purpose of
education.

Formation and Development

Know thyself. These words were inscribed in the Temple of Apollo at Delphi in ancient Greece. Nobel laureate Bob Dylan mused: "All I can do is be me—whoever that is."[1] Self-knowledge isn't the easiest thing to come by. It's a lot of work.

Developing self-knowledge is or should be a prime purpose of education. In northern Europe, it's called *Bildung.*[2] The German word *Bildung* is a cognate with the English word *building.* A good education gives students the tools that they need to *build up* their own identities. Only in this way, the tradition of *Bildung* tells us, can people break free from the constraints of custom and social conformity. Wilhelm von Humboldt, founder of the University of Berlin and a champion of *Bildung,* wrote that the point of *Bildung* was to "*build yourself,* and influence others through who you are."[3] *Bildung* is about human development across the life span. It is a necessary complement to academic learning.

At Boston College, the purpose of human development is understood in terms of a related idea: *formative education.* This is a central part of the ethos, curriculum, and pedagogy of the whole institution, which sees itself not just as qualifying graduates but as developing or forming whole human beings in and for society. In *formative education,* students are pushed to develop their skills of critical reflection by probing life's most important challenges. This begins with an orientation lecture where three questions are presented:

1. *What gives you joy?*

2. *Are you good at it now, or could you get good at it?*

3. *Does the world need it?*

Throughout their undergraduate education, Boston College students are given opportunities to attend seminars, go on off-campus retreats, and participate in service-learning trips in which they reflect on these three questions. Faculty and other staff are invited to pursue these activities, too. Every person is encouraged to undertake their own quest to give their lives meaning and purpose, by following their own conscience, and by clarifying their aspirations about what is most important to them, and why.

The quest for meaning and identity commences very early in life. In Ireland, developing identity is one of the four foundations of the early childhood curriculum.[4] Educators in the francophone

(French-language) schools in Ontario have worked on Franco-Ontarian identity issues for years to make sure that their minority culture is protected and preserved, even as the school's population becomes increasingly globalized.

Programs such as these are grounded in the principles of the United Nations Convention on the Rights of the Child (UNCRC). Ratified in 1989, this affirmed "that all children have the right to an education that lays a foundation for the rest of their lives, maximizes their ability, *and respects their family, cultural and other identities and languages*" (our emphasis).[5] In the UNCRC, identity formation is *a fundamental human right for all children in all countries.* The UNCRC sets out the rights that all children have, to help fulfill their potential. These include rights relating to health and education, leisure and play, fair and equal treatment, protection from exploitation, and, not least, *the right to be heard.*

Every country around the world except one has ratified the UNCRC. Scotland has gone further by enshrining the convention into law as far as the wider parameters of the United Kingdom's Westminster government permit. In 2021, the Scottish Parliament unanimously passed the "United Nations Convention on the Rights of the Child (Incorporation) (Scotland) Bill."[6] The United States, on the other hand, has still not even signed the UNCRC. This is because 29 U.S. states have laws that violate the convention's Article 37, which prohibits life imprisonment without parole for crimes committed by those under 18 years old.[7]

The Organisation for Economic Co-operation and Development (OECD), meanwhile, has moved beyond its focus on international test results to develop global competencies that promote those aspects of a "quality education" that are contained in the 17 sustainable development goals of the UN. According to the OECD, "the first domain of knowledge for global competence relates to the manifold expressions of culture and intercultural relations," which can "*help young people to become more aware of their own cultural identity*" (our emphasis) and "avoid categorizing people through single markers of identity."[8] Global competence, according to the OECD, should enable young people "to retain their cultural identity" while respecting "the cultural values and beliefs of people around them."[9]

Through models of human formation, government policies, and the advocacy of organizations like the UN and the OECD, identity is an increasingly prominent issue for schools and school systems around the world.

How people develop their identities is not a new question. Many of the world's great sagas and legends describe the inner struggles that people feel when one set of loyalties conflicts with another. Fables and folk tales like Cinderella, Beauty and the Beast, and the movie *Frozen* are about losses of innocence, encounters with evil, and transitions into adulthood, with a few archetypal aspects of romance thrown in along the way.

For almost 100 years, social scientists have explained more fully how human identities evolve and develop over time through *psychological development*, *life passages*, and *generational shifts*. These are the three aspects of identity development we address next.

Psychological Development

In his 1950 Pulitzer Prize–winning book, *Childhood and Society*, Harvard University psychologist Erik Erikson described eight major identity transitions or crises that all people negotiate as they go through life.[10] For Erikson, a crisis was "a turning point, a crucial period of increased vulnerability and heightened potential."[11] Erikson's theories of identity crises were insightful and reassuring for those who wondered why young people seemed to be so conflicted at the time. Since then, his theories of identity crises, and their corresponding stages, have been taught in psychology classes all over the world. Figure 2.1 details these eight stages.

Erikson's stages have become widespread parts of common sense. We all know about the "terrible twos" of the second stage, about teenagers' desperate desire to be included in the most popular peer groups, and about people's longing for intimacy and commitment in their 20s and 30s, for example. Almost every stage involves struggling with negative emotions and personal setbacks and trying to tip the scales toward growth and renewal.

As we were writing this book, one of Andy's grandsons, Jackson, was approaching his 10th birthday. "Well, then," he announced abruptly, "only a few days left being a child!" It was as if he had read Erikson's model and decided to implement it. Jackson was moving through Erikson's industry versus inferiority stage. No longer a dependent

Through models of human formation, government policies, and the advocacy of organizations like the UN and the OECD, identity is an increasingly prominent issue for schools and school systems around the world.

Figure 2.1 Erik Erikson's Eight Stages of Psychological Development

1. *Birth to roughly 18 months:*

   Infants seek *trust* and attachment to their caregivers. If nurturance and safety are continuously provided, they learn to overcome the threat of *mistrust*, and the path is cleared for further healthy development.

2. *18 months to 3 years:*

   The child strives to develop an *autonomous will* so that it learns it is safe and proper to "be oneself" in a world made up of other people.[12] This sense of independence is critical to healthy development. Without it, a child experiences *doubt* and *shame*.

3. *3 to 6 years:*

   The child aspires to exercise *initiative* and undertake freely chosen projects through increasingly elaborate forms of play. If adults thwart the child's natural desire to explore their environments, feelings of *guilt* will ensue, experienced as "a new and powerful estrangement."[13]

4. *6 to 11 years:*

   There is an expansion of children's social world. Through their *industry*, children develop a sense of mastery over their environment. If this sense of accomplishment is stunted, they experience a "sense of *inferiority*" that holds back their maturation.[14]

5. *11 to 18 years:*

   Adolescents struggle between *identity consolidation* and *role confusion*. They "temporarily over-identify" with a chosen peer group and "perversely test each other's capacity to pledge fidelity."[15] Bullying can increase, not only to intimidate victims but also to impress peers.

6. *19 to 40 years:*

   In young adulthood, people either establish *intimacy* with partners or experience *isolation* and loneliness. A lasting sense of stability is or is not established. This has profound consequences for the last two stages.

7. *41 to 65 years:*

   Adults struggle to attain *generativity*, "the concern for establishing and guiding the next generation."[16] The alternative is a "pervading sense of *stagnation*" marked by "personal impoverishment" and a sense of bitterness at missed opportunities and squandered talent.[17]

8. *66 years until death:*

   This can be a time when people "gradually ripen the fruit of the seven stages" into a fully formed sense of personal *integrity*.[18] Failure to achieve this results in *despair*, which "expresses the feeling that time is too short for the attempt to start another life and to try out alternate roads to integrity."[19]

Figure 2.1   Erik Erikson's Eight Stages of Psychological Development (Continued)

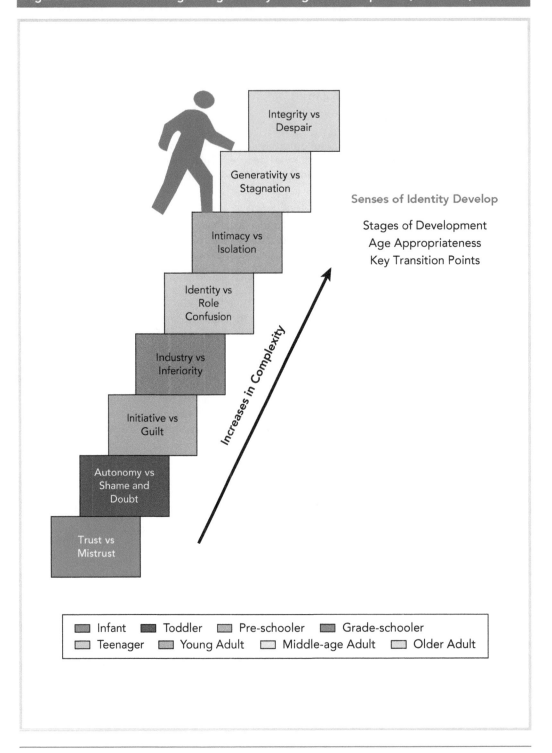

Source: Erikson, 1968

child, he was accepting—even welcoming—the moment when work, action, and affecting things around him would enable him to assert his autonomy.

Then, as if he was deliberately putting this self-revelation into action, a couple of days later, Jackson invited his granddad out on his paddleboard. Andy sat on the back of the board while Jackson confidently steered them out into the lake (Figure 2.2) and around to a couple of his secret coves. This was the first time Jackson had ever taken the leading role with Andy on any outdoor activity or adventure. It was a wonderful moment. It was also a poignant one.

We are on Erikson's staircase of identity development too. Almost at the very top, in fact. Jackson is taking his granddad out on his paddleboard now. In 10 or 15 years, he may be driving him to the mall. The stages are connected to each other. Eager and fit as we feel to keep pushing ahead, we also find ourselves paying more and more attention to people behind us on the staircase, to help them find a good path and enable *their* development as part of our own generativity.

For now, if we take care of the likes of Jackson, then hopefully they will, in turn, start to take us with them on their metaphorical paddleboards.

Figure 2.2   Jackson and Andy on Their Paddleboard Adventure

Like rising stars performing alongside distinguished older actors whose brief cameos dignify the rest of the cast's work, our professional grandchildren will hopefully show us off to their students and colleagues, filling our twilight years with warmth. It's up to us and those we teach, mentor, and support whether life will turn out to be more like Led Zeppelin's "Stairway to Heaven" or AC/DC's "Highway to Hell."

> It's up to us and those we teach, mentor, and support whether life will turn out to be more like Led Zeppelin's "Stairway to Heaven" or AC/DC's "Highway to Hell."

Although Erikson's ideas have everyday acceptance now, they were highly controversial at first. One of Erikson's mentors when he was at Yale University in the 1930s had been the legendary anthropologist Margaret Mead. Her groundbreaking book, *Coming of Age in Samoa*, captivated readers with its analysis of how very different cultures dealt with people's life stages and transitions.[20] Beneath and across all the cultural differences, Mead inspired Erikson to observe recognizable patterns in ritual celebrations of childbirth, naming ceremonies, the end of childhood, marriage, or a death in the family, for example.

How people deal with coming of age is not the same in all cultures, of course. The universal nature of these life transitions is sometimes overemphasized. So, too, is the rigidity of the stages. "It is utterly false and cruelly arbitrary to put all the play into childhood, all the work into middle age, and all the regrets into old age," Mead said.[21] Erickson's staircase is a vertical pathway that people can go up and down, and get on and off, at any time. It's not an escalator that traps them on an inexorable journey at a predetermined pace, the moment they step onto it.

Life Passages

By the 1960s, Erikson had left Yale and moved on to Harvard University, where one of his associates was another psychologist, Daniel Levinson. Greatly influenced by Erikson, Levinson undertook a biographical interview study of 40 men in midlife to understand the stages and transitions that they went through as they progressed through their life cycle. He popularized the idea of midlife crisis. Levinson was an early advocate of positive psychological development. People didn't have to atrophy after adolescence was over, he believed. Rather, all the way through life and into old age, their identities evolved in ways that presented challenging but nonetheless achievable transitions. They did so in four overlapping "eras each lasting roughly twenty-five years" (see Figure 2.3).[22]

Levinson produced two key works. The first, in 1978, was *The Seasons of a Man's Life*.[23] After he was criticized for neglecting women's development, Levinson undertook a second series of interviews to check whether his four overlapping eras were as applicable to women as to

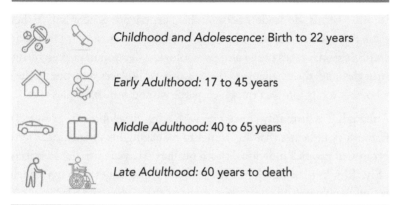

Figure 2.3 Evolving Identities Over Time

Childhood and Adolescence: Birth to 22 years

Early Adulthood: 17 to 45 years

Middle Adulthood: 40 to 65 years

Late Adulthood: 60 years to death

Source: Rattle icon by iStock.com/Priyanka gupta; skateboard icon by iStock.com/ Oksana Sazhnieva; house icon by iStock.com/rambo182; parent and child icon by iStock.com/appleuzr; car icon by iStock.com/Maksym Rudoi; briefcase icon by iStock.com/Stakes; person with cane icon by iStock.com/surfupvector; person in wheelchair icon by iStock.com/Miray Celebi Kaba.

men. In 1996, two years after his death, *The Seasons of a Woman's Life* was published by his wife, Judy.[24]

"The life structure develops through a relatively orderly sequence of age-linked periods during the adult years," Levinson argued.[25] Each stage had qualities that have to do with the character of living at a particular time and with a culturally defined set of challenges. For example, he claimed, the midlife crisis seemed to be pronounced among his interviewees regardless of whether they were male or female, professional or working-class. Although there were some minor areas of gender differences, Levinson still found striking similarities in the life cycle, regardless of gender.

The research on adult life development has had an enormous influence on the study of teachers' and leaders' lives and career stages in education. Educators have identity issues too. They also go through life stages and transitions. The most systematic work on how life and career stages impact teachers and their effectiveness has been carried out in the United Kingdom and Europe.[26] Here, we learn that if teachers persist and remain after the first few years, they are likely to be most effective between 8 and 23 years on the job: typically, between about 30 years old and their mid- to late 40s. It's after this point, in Levinson's final stage and Erickson's last two stages, that teachers are most vulnerable to losing commitment and effectiveness.

Leaders can make a big difference here. Do they let teachers carry on doing the same thing, year after year, until they get bored and weary, or do they challenge them to teach new topics or different classes, to lead innovation teams, or to mentor new members into the profession? In other words, do leaders help teachers experience generativity rather than the much-criticized blight of late-career stagnation? Levinson's and Erickson's stages of life and psychological development present the struggles and the challenges. But it's our workplaces and our leaders who have a huge impact on which paths we and our colleagues take.

Although it is primarily concerned with adult development, Levinson's framework indicates that difficulties in managing life's transitions aren't because of people's individual shortcomings. They are inevitable aspects of healthy human development. Moreover, the stages through which young people pass in the development of their selves and identities are closely related to the stages through which their parents, grandparents, and teachers at school are passing too. As we shall see shortly, the development of young people's identities is an intergenerational phenomenon, as well as a purely psychological one.

Both Erikson's and Levinson's work have had immense influence on people's thinking about life and human development, inside schools and in the wider world. But both men had a significant Achilles' heel: *women*—or their failure to address women's identities properly. Erikson called his framework *Eight Stages of Man*. Levinson's early work was exclusively focused on men's development. Even his later attempts to address differences in girls' and women's development explained them away as deviations from the supposedly normal male path to independence and autonomy.

Also working in the mid-1970s, journalist Gail Sheehy published a *New York Times* bestseller: *Passages: Predictable Crises of Adult Life*.[27] Sheehy's interest in life transitions was partly inspired by time she spent as a graduate student working under Margaret Mead, who was then in her eighth decade. Sheehy conducted 115 interviews with men and women from 18 to 65 years old. Finding that many of them seemed unsettled, she turned to various intellectual sources of influence that included Erickson, Levinson, and the Canadian psychoanalyst Elliott Jaques, who invented but had not popularized the concept of midlife crisis.

Sheehy's distinctive contribution was to take the stages of girls' and women's maturation and development seriously from the start. While women, like men, struggled to balance intimacy and isolation in middle age, for example, she found that women's socialization prepared them to be caregivers as mothers and wives, so their challenges had to do not so much with asserting autonomy as with the quality of their relationships. Likewise, the dichotomy that men faced in late middle age between stagnation and generativity in their careers was experienced differently by women, whose supportive roles in their families often entailed putting others first, which led them to neglect their own flourishing. While women, like men, could overcome these difficulties in what Sheehy later termed a "second adulthood" that followed the midlife crisis, this was in no way guaranteed, especially if there was a failure to understand how power and gender roles shape life histories.[28]

There were bitter rivalries between Levinson and Sheehy of the kind that sometimes accompany writers who are aware of each other's work, but where one publishes a book and gets public acclaim before the other. Sheehy was influenced by Levinson, but she still released her book first, in 1976—two years before Levinson published his own. Sheehy acknowledged Levinson's influence, but on seeing Sheehy—the journalist—bring out her bestseller first, Levinson didn't return the favor when he eventually went to press in 1978.

What united Mead, Erikson, Levinson, and Sheehy was the conviction that people around the world go through recognizable stages of development that have their own identifiable challenges. All of them, however, became targets for critics who charged them with neglecting what makes cultures historically and geographically distinct, compared to what they have in common. Adolescence, some say, didn't really become established as a separate phase of development between childhood and adulthood, even in Western societies, until after the Second World War.[29] Young people's development in many East and South Asian cultures that emphasize social and family harmony is in some ways profoundly different from the West with its greater emphases on independence and individualism.[30] In Italy, which ranks at the top of the world in well-being on the Bloomberg Global Health Index, men stay at home with their parents well into their 30s or until they get married—longer than men in almost every other modern society.[31] Women's family and work roles, and women's ability to control their own fertility and life choices, underwent profound transformations in the 20th century. Not surprisingly, given the times of these books' publication, gay and lesbian relationships and identities do not appear in any of these authors' works at all, even though there has been informed conjecture that Mead herself may have been in a long-term lesbian relationship in her later years.[32] Growing up is not the same for everyone, nor are the ways in which cultures manage adulthood.

Yet, the phases and stages through which children and young people move matter everywhere. The responsibility of educators is to be sensitive to local cultures that affect their classes and to different groups of students within those classes. This can help them guide their students through each stage of development, so they come out all the better for the experience on the other side. Differences, diversities, and what we will later recognize as forms of intersectionality are all important, but, in *the Age of Identity*, the universal tasks of human development and formation in modern society matter everywhere too. It is essential that teachers are ready, willing, and eager to assume their responsibility for human formation so they can help every student learn how to be, and how to be better, within their own cultures, at every stage of their development.

Generational Shifts

Developing an identity over time isn't a process that is simply biological, or a function of age or chronology. Nor is identity development a universal or timeless process that can be easily compared across groups or epochs. Although developing a sense of self and building an identity over time happens within all cultures and societies, it is not as if cultures and societies are static, while individuals are not. The individual *and* the group are both engaged in dynamic processes of development.

Teachers hitting middle age and later life know all too well that every year they get older, their students seem to stay pretty much the same. But they don't always grasp that adolescence isn't the same as when *they* were teenagers several decades ago. School leaders may not see that new teacher recruits aren't simple rewinds of their younger professional selves, either. We need to understand that what adolescence looks like is not just a result of it being a period between childhood and adulthood. It is also a feature of the generation into which young people are born that in many ways comes to shape their entire lives.

When we were working on the final sections of this book, we sat down with an undergraduate class Dennis was teaching called *The Educational Conversation*. Our topic was COVID-19 and its impact on young people. One young woman, who was studying neuroscience, drew affirmation when she pointed out that as we were all coming out of the pandemic, people ahead of them in age and career terms were starting to revert to something like the life they had before. They had a point of reference to return to, as they had already been able to develop a generational identity.

She and her peers, she pointed out, had no such prior point of reference. Her brain was still developing, she said, and COVID-19 was part of that process, shaping how she would be, and what she would become, for the rest of her life. The experiences in particular places and times that teenagers have as their brains are still forming influence them forever. This is what generations are about.

It is essential that teachers are ready, willing, and eager to assume their responsibility for human formation so they can help every student learn how to be, and how to be better, within their own cultures, at every stage of their development.

The idea of generations was invented in 1928, by Karl Mannheim, a Hungarian-German sociologist who fled to the United Kingdom before the commencement of World War II. Mannheim explained generations in sociological terms as age cohorts whose shared experiences in youth were subsequently carried through the ensuing decades of their lives. He was especially interested in what he called "crystallizing agents" or defining events that were distinctive to a rising generation.[33] These influenced how each generational cohort understood itself, and then shaped the wider society as it aged and as members of each generational cohort moved into positions of leadership.

In 1997, William Strauss and Neil Howe developed Mannheim's insights into a fully fledged theory of generational changes. In *The Fourth Turning*, they argued that generations typically span about 20 years.[34] Like Mannheim, they said that each rising youth cohort experiences a "Great Event" that gives it its unique "generational persona."[35] In modern U.S. terms, they identified four generations spanning the 1950s to the 2000s.

FOUR GENERATIONS SPANNING THE 1950s–2000s

1. The *Silent Generation* of the 1950s built a period of economic and organizational stability after World War II.

2. The *Baby Boom Generation* in the 1960s and 1970s saw revolutions in gender equity, youth rebellion, and civil rights.

3. *Generation X* in the 1980s and 1990s grew up amidst a great economic unraveling, and became individualistic, market-oriented, and calculative as a result.

4. The *Millennial Generation* or *Generation Y* in the 2000s faced mounting crises of growing social inequality, climate change, and massive global movements of refugees.

In *Millennials Rising*, published in 2000, Strauss and Howe predicted that this new generation would "manifest a wide array of positive social habits that older Americans no longer associate with youth, including a new focus on teamwork, achievement, modesty, and good conduct."[36]

Will the optimistic predictions of Strauss and Howe come true with the passage of time? Millennials, and Generation Z that followed them, have shown in their online and in-person lives that they can be fully engaged with the world around them. In the wake of Brexit, for example, there has been a surge in applications to study political science at U.K. universities.[37] It is the young who have led the global climate strike called *Fridays for Future* that has pushed leaders and members of the public around the world to act.[38] Fully 70% of all U.S. youth responded to one survey indicating that they had participated in Black Lives Matter protests or deliberations after the murders of George Floyd and Breonna Taylor in 2020.[39] Anticipating these high levels of civic engagement, Strauss and Howe described Millennials as "the next Great Generation" that would be keen to take on the mantle of leadership and to tackle the challenges confronting all of us.

Not everyone is this optimistic. Psychologists like Jean Twenge, who wrote *iGen: Why Today's Super-Connected Kids Are Growing Up Less Rebellious, More Tolerant, Less Happy—and Completely Unprepared for Adulthood—and What That Means for the Rest of Us*, are concerned about increases in technological addictiveness, egocentricity, and narcissism among the young.[40] Strauss and Howe did not foresee a world in which teenagers would have ubiquitous access to smartphones and social media platforms like Instagram, Snapchat, WhatsApp, and TikTok, which they use for hours at a time every day. Nor did they anticipate a world in which online anxiety, cyberbullying, and digital distraction would become ever-present dangers.

Are we entering a world of increased social engagement, more technological addiction and distraction, or some combination of the two? We don't completely know yet how these two battling forces will resolve themselves, but the most important insight is that teenagers are not just younger than their teachers, and new generations aren't just defective versions of older ones. Generations in general, and each generation in particular, matter in their own terms.

In *Generational Identity, Educational Change, and School Leadership*, State University of New York at Buffalo professor Corrie Stone-Johnson describes how Generation X teachers she studied didn't mind the standardization and testing that their Baby Boomer peers despised.[41] They appreciated frameworks and guidelines that meant they didn't have to make up the curriculum all by themselves. Compared to their Baby Boomer colleagues who exhausted themselves by sacrificing evenings, holidays, and weekends for the sake of their mission to transform young people's lives, Generation X teachers valued a more balanced life. They performed their jobs professionally, but protected their personal time by pursuing other interests, too.

Generational consultants Jennifer Abrams and Valerie von Frank argue that people need coaching on how to talk and act cross-generationally.[42] Teachers who are also parents and who are assertive about which

> Teenagers are not just younger than their teachers, and new generations aren't just defective versions of older ones. Generations in general, and each generation in particular, matter in their own terms.

after-school meetings they will and will not attend, so as not to encroach on family time, are not simply slackers, but professionals who want their leaders to consider their own needs for a balanced life. Generation X teachers may not devote endless extra hours discussing and reflecting on their mission and their practice, but if they are given a purposeful task to complete as a team, they will dispatch it with awesome efficiency.

Today's students do not need to be harangued by older generations about their digital devices being instruments of the devil. They do not want to hear that sexual health is only about safety, and never about pleasure. Grit and sacrifice will not engage them. Endless examinations and tests may simply drive them to "escape from learning," in the words of Japanese professor Manabu Sato.[43]

Will today's rising generations step up to engage with the world? Will this be a significant part of their identity? In the United States, election turnout in 2022 among 18- to 29-year-olds was the second highest it has been in 30 years.[44] One global survey after another is showing how young people aged between the late teens and mid-30s are worried about climate change, anxious about war, outraged by violence, and fearful about the future. [45] They want to stop the world, not to get off but to put it back on its axis. Young people's evolving identities today aren't just about maturation and growth. They are bound up with young people wanting to be agents of their time. The development of student identity is a *social*, *cultural*, and *historical* question, not just an inner *psychological* one.

> The development of student identity, in other words, is a *social*, *cultural*, and *historical* question, not just an inner *psychological* one.

IDENTITIES OVER TIME

Taken together, theories of psychological development, life passages, and generational identities give educators powerful new ways to see their students and themselves. A rebellious early adolescent might not be challenging your authority just for the fun of it; instead, they might be trying to establish a new identity in which prestige among peers takes precedence over everything else. Students scrolling through their screens during class might be checking out Instagram friends, but they might also be checking up on you to see if what you have been teaching them is true!

It's also wise to explore where you are in your own life's passages. Being hard on yourself or on colleagues who lose energy in managing the transition from the boundless enthusiasm of the unencumbered beginning teacher to the midcareer professional with a family to raise, a mortgage to pay, and aging parents to care for is not only damaging to well-being; it also fails to acknowledge the role that life passages play in shaping your own and your colleagues' development. Likewise, reflecting on when you were born, and on what critical issues your generation has confronted, can help all of us to rethink our relationships with members of other generations and the kinds of conversations we have with them.

These theories of identity all portray it as something that emerges, unfolds, and develops over time. It moves forward across the life cycle, whether it ends up bitter and twisted or harmonious and integrated. Yet we now know that identity is even more complicated and contradictory than this. We behave differently online than offline. We are perceived differently by our family than our work associates. Sometimes, young people these days aren't even sure what their identity is. Some identities are things we can celebrate and show off to others—the top of the class, the tech guru, the homecoming queen. Other identities are ones we sometimes feel pressed to hide—the poverty of our family, our struggles with mental health, or being LGBTQ+. Our identities can be sources of pride or shame. They are complex and complicated, and increasingly, they are also controversial. These aspects of identity are the subject of our next chapters.

Notes

1. PBS. (2016, May 23). Favorite quotes from American master Bob Dylan. *American Masters*. https://www.pbs.org/wnet/americanmasters/blog/best-bob -dylan-quotes/
2. Herdt, J. A. (2019). *Forming humanity: Redeeming the German* Bildung *tradition*. University of Chicago Press.
3. Mattson, P. (Ed.). (2017). *Wilhelm von Humboldt: Briefe Juli 1795–Juni 1797*. De Gruyter.
4. For information on the Irish early childhood curriculum, go to the website of the Irish National Council for Curriculum and Assessment at https://curriculum online.ie/Early-Childhood/.
5. United Nations. (1989). *Convention on the rights of the child*. Office of the High Commissioner for Human Rights. https://www.ohchr.org/en/instruments -mechanisms/instruments/convention-rights-child
6. Scottish Parliament. (2023). *United Nations convention on the rights of the child (incorporation) (Scotland) bill*. https://www.parliament.scot/bills-and-laws/bills/ united-nations-convention-on-the-rights-of-the-child-incorporation-scotland-bill

7. Mehta, S. (2015, November 20). There's only one country that hasn't ratified the convention on children's rights: The US. *ACLU News and Commentary*. https://www.aclu.org/news/human-rights/theres-only-one-country-hasnt -ratified-convention-childrens

8. OECD Programme for International Student Assessment. (2018). *Preparing youth for an inclusive and sustainable world: The OECD PISA global compe- tence framework*. https://www.oecd.org/education/Global-competency-for-an -inclusive-world.pdf

9. Ibid.

10. Erikson, E. H. (1963). *Childhood and society*. Norton.

11. Erikson, E. H. (1968). *Identity: Youth and crisis*. Norton, p. 96.

12. Ibid., p. 107.

13. Ibid., p. 119.

14. Ibid., p. 114.

15. Ibid., p. 132; Erikson, *Childhood*, p. 262.

16. Erikson, *Childhood*, p. 267.

17. Ibid.

18. Ibid., p. 268.

19. Erikson, *Identity*, p. 140.

20. Mead, M. (2001). *Coming of age in Samoa: A psychological study of primitive youth for western civilization*. Perennial Classics. (Original work published 1928)

21. Mead quoted in Baughman, M. D. (1958). *Teachers' treasury for every occasion*. Prentice-Hall, p. 69.

22. Levinson, D. J. (1978). *The seasons of a man's life*. Ballantine, p. 18.

23. Levinson, D. J. (1978). *The seasons of a man's life*. Ballantine.

24. Levinson, D. J., & Levinson, J. D. (1996). *The seasons of a woman's life*. Ballantine.

25. Levinson, D. J. (1986). A conception of adult development. *American Psychologist*, *41*(1), 3–13, quote from p. 7.

26. Day, C., & Gu, Q. (2010). *The new lives of teachers: Teacher quality and school development*. Routledge; Day, C., Stobart, G., Sammons, P., Kington, A., & Gu, Q. (2007). *Teachers matter: Connecting lives, work, and effectiveness*. Open University Press.

27. Sheehy, G. (1976). *Passages: Predictable crises of adult life*. Dutton.

28. Sheehy, G. (2006). *Passages: Predictable crises of adult life* (30th anniversary ed.). Dutton, p. xxiii.

29. Fasick, F. A. (1994). On the "invention" of adolescence. *Journal of Early Adolescence*, *14*(1), 6–23.

30. Liu, P. (2017). Comparison between Chinese and Canadian transformational school leadership practices: A cultural analysis. *International Studies in Educational Administration*, *45*(1), 38–54.

31. Lu, W., & Del Giudice, V. (2017, March 20). *Italy's struggling economy has world's healthiest people*. Bloomberg. https://www.bloomberg.com/news/ articles/2017-03-20/italy-s-struggling-economy-has-world-s-healthiest -people#xj4y7vzkg; Vogt, A. (2012, September 19). Third of Italian adults live with their parents, report finds. *The Guardian*. https://www.theguardian.com/ world/2012/sep/19/third-italians-live-with-parents

32. See Bateson, M. C. (2001). *With a daughter's eye: A memoir of Margaret Mead and Gregory Bateson*. Perennial.

33. Kecskemeti, P. (Ed.). (1952). *Karl Mannheim: Essays*. Routledge, pp. 276–322, quote from p. 310. (Original work published 1927)

34. Strauss, W., & Howe, N. (1997). *The fourth turning: An American prophecy*. Broadway.

35. Ibid., p. 58.

36. Howe, N., & Strauss, W. (2000). *Millennials rising: The next great generation*. Vintage, p. 4.

37. Wheeler, B. (2019, October 27). *Brexit sparks boom in applications for politics courses*. BBC. https://www.bbc.com/news/uk-politics-50071242

38. Gayle, D. (2022, March 25). Fridays for Future climate strikes resume across the world. *The Guardian*. https://www.theguardian.com/environment/2022/mar/25/fridays-for-future-school-climate-strikes-resume

39. Hurst, K. (2022, June 15). *US teens more likely than adults to support the Black Lives Matter movement*. Pew Research Center. https://www.pewresearch.org/fact-tank/2022/06/15/u-s-teens-are-more-likely-than-adults-to-support-the-black-lives-matter-movement/

40. Twenge, J. M. (2018). *iGen: Why today's super-connected kids are growing up less rebellious, more tolerant, less happy—and completely unprepared for adulthood—and what that means for the rest of us*. Atria.

41. Stone-Johnson, C. (2016). *Generational identity, educational change, and school leadership*. Routledge.

42. Abrams, J., & von Frank, V. A. (2014). *The multigenerational workplace: Communicate, collaborate, and create community*. Corwin.

43. Sato, M. (2011). Imagining neo-liberalism and the hidden realities of the politics of reform: Teachers and students in a globalized Japan. In D. B. Blake & J. Rappleye (Eds.), *Reimagining Japanese education: Borders, transfers, circulations, and the comparative* (pp. 225–246). Symposium, quote from p. 226.

44. Center for Information Research on Civic Learning and Engagement. (2022). *Youth voter turnout and impact in the 2022 midterm elections*. Tisch College of Civic Life, Tufts University. https://circle.tufts.edu/sites/default/files/2022-12/early_data_youth_vote_report.pdf

45. Skopeliti, C., & Gecsoyler, S. (2023, March 23). "Terrified for my future": Climate change takes heavy toll on young people's mental health. *The Guardian*. https://www.theguardian.com/environment/2023/mar/30/terrified-for-my-future-climate-crisis-takes-heavy-toll-on-young-peoples-mental-health

CHAPTER 3

The Self and Others

Each to each a looking glass

Reflect the other that doth pass.

—Charles Horton Cooley (1902)[1]

Our selves are not things *within* us. They are processes that evolve *between* and *among* us.

The Social Self

How have any of us come to be the ways we are? Were we, like the title of Lady Gaga's album, simply *born this way*?[2] Or did we will ourselves into being stronger, braver, more charming, more likable, or whatever? Or did other people have an influence on us too?

Our families, friends, colleagues, and networks can have a powerful effect on who we are. Can you recall a pivotal moment with a parent, a grandparent, or another caregiver when an encouraging word, or a stern rebuke, made an imprint on you? Perhaps you'll always remember the unshakable bond you forged with a friend when you both faced down bullies in the schoolyard together. And if you joined the #WomenEd grassroots network in education, do you feel 10% braver now because of the support and solidarity you receive from it?[3]

Today, it's common to think of the self in individual and psychological terms. Open an issue of *Self* magazine, with a readership of over 5 million, and you're treated to a cornucopia of recommendations about what you can do to improve your looks, enhance your diet, and advance your career. Enter the term *self* into the browser of your online bookstore, and it's more of the same. Titles like *Best Self* and *The Self-Love Workbook* regard the self as the individual.[4] So too do popular movements that promote self-help and self-care. There's even a trend toward *sologamy* or marrying yourself.[5] Why marry someone else, with all their quirks and flaws, when the best choice available is staring right back at you in the mirror?

Another way of thinking about what it means to be a human being, though, is the *social self*. Here, our selves are not things *within* us. They are processes that evolve *between* and *among* us. The classic sociological theory of the self and its formation belongs to a field known as *symbolic interactionism* that started in Chicago in the 1930s. It addressed how human selves, identities, and cultures are formed through interactions with others, and through how these interactions reflect our selves back to us. As long ago as 1902, Charles H. Cooley had already depicted what he called a "looking-glass self," in which others serve as mirrors for the development of our own identities.[6] In this view, we come to see ourselves in terms of how other people respond to us—especially those who matter to us, like family members, colleagues, teachers, and friends.

The foundational theorist of symbolic interactionism was George Herbert Mead. In his 1934 book, *Mind, Self and Society*, Mead distinguished between the driven *I* (rather like Sigmund Freud's *ego* and *id*) and the social *me* that was built through other people's perceptions and feedback.[7] Over time, the symbolic interactionist research of the

Chicago School of Sociology focused on the identities, cultures, and careers that ordinary people developed. Occupations and careers such as carpentry, funeral directing, medicine, policing, criminality, and house cleaning, as well as activities such as playing jazz or taking drugs, had their own cultures with which people identified.

The same was true of teaching as an occupation. In different ways, Willard Waller in the 1930s and Dan Lortie in the 1970s, who both did graduate degrees in Chicago, asked the same question: What does teaching do to teachers? What is it about how teaching is organized that shapes teachers' identities?[8]

The Chicago School found that occupational cultures had common norms and ways of behaving. They had a shared purpose that was shaped by the nature of their work. They understood that there were ways to do and not to do things. There were implicit and explicit pressures to keep people in line. Group cultures are evident everywhere: in communities and workplaces, in clubs and societies, in schools and universities, in gangs and crews. People feel they belong to them and form attachments to what they represent, occupationally and socially. In many ways, who we are at work is shaped by who we work with and what we do together.

Former Boston College professor Everett Hughes was a central member of the Chicago School. He studied how good people struggle to develop a positive sense of identity when they perform what he famously called "dirty work," like burying bodies or disposing of trash.[9] He coauthored one of the Chicago School's best-known studies—*Boys in White*—that documented the unique culture of medical students.[10] With his Canadian wife, Helen MacGill Hughes, and Irwin Deutscher, he also conducted a complementary study of the nursing profession.[11] In 1958, Hughes set out one of the first and most important sociological explanations of the meaning of work in *Men and Their Work*.[12]

Unusually among his Chicago School peers, Hughes also took a great interest in how people's selves and identities were bound up with and affected by race and racism, and by what we now call "marginalization" in society. Influenced by his wife, he developed an intense interest in French Canadian culture. In the 1930s, he studied how the minority English-speaking population in a small town in Quebec that he called Cantonville suppressed French culture and values with a business-focused Protestantism that accompanied and drove industrialization.[13] His book became a classic of Canadian sociology. Its impact was so great that, in 1963, Hughes was asked to carry out a study for the Canadian Royal Commission on Bilingualism and Biculturalism.

Hughes's work in Canada paralleled another investigation he conducted of the Catholic labor movement and its relationship with Protestant managers in 1930s Germany.[14] In both cases, Hughes was concerned with the interaction and conflict between majority or dominant cultures and minority cultures and movements. For him, the formation of the self through relationships was not just the small-scale phenomenon of occupations or lifestyle subcultures that it was for many of his Chicago School counterparts. It was also part of how power was exercised and of how subgroups defined by language, race, and religion were subjugated and persecuted in deeply unequal societies.

What do these ideas mean for educators? Waller and Lortie showed that schools have their work cultures too, and that these shape teachers' identities. But the work on teachers' identities didn't stop there. Research in the 1980s and 1990s revealed how high school teachers develop different subject-matter identities as instructors of social studies, languages, mathematics, or music, respectively.

Students also create cultures and subcultures that contribute to their identities. To build a sense of belonging, U.S. students form cliques of nerdy and preppy kids, skaters and jocks, or, more ominously, Crips and Bloods. In Japan, there are other kinds of youth cultures including anime, punk, cute *kawaii*, and rebellious *yankii*. In his 1968 book coauthored with fellow Chicago School sociologists Howard Becker and Blanche Geer, *Making the Grade: The Academic Side of College Life*, Hughes unearthed a contradictory college culture that granted students autonomy over social and extramural affairs, but subjected them to an endless chase after grades and improved grade point averages.[15] Their analysis of the pressures that this placed upon students, and their struggles to resolve them, still rings true.

These cultures are sources and expressions of identity. They provide a sense of belonging that is defined by the students themselves in ways that are beyond the total control of their teachers. They are important for educators to understand and to engage with, not only in their own right, but also because of how they interact with the official structure of the school.

Back in the 1960s, Andy's U.K. namesake and future colleague, David Hargreaves, studied what happened to students when they were streamed or tracked into different secondary school classes according to their measured attainment.[16] Over time, two very different student cultures evolved. The top two streams were characterized by *academic* cultures in which students valued hard work, achievement, and complying with school norms. In the bottom streams, by contrast, a *delinquescent* culture prevailed. This culture took everything the academic culture valued and inverted it so that status rose in association with coarse language, bad behavior, and lack of achievement.

Researchers of youth cultures have repeatedly stressed how rebellious or resistant identities are not just expressions of failures to succeed in the formal culture of academic success. They are deliberate, alternative ways of gaining status, satisfaction, and engagement in school instead. They are conscious constructions, not default options. Most people feel they need to belong to something bigger than themselves. If their school does not offer this to them, they seek recognition elsewhere, in other ways. If the school is not connected to the community, the gang will set itself against the school.

In schools and societies, it feels better to belong to something than not. *Learning to live together* is about developing this sense of belonging. But not any kind of belonging or togetherness will do. Neo-Nazi youth groups, soccer hooligans, criminal gangs, xenophobic nationalists, elitist and exclusionary college fraternities and sororities, "mean girls," and bullying boys—these are not the kinds of belonging that schools should be cultivating or settling for.

> If the school is not connected to the community, the gang will set itself against the school.

Identity and belonging are intertwined with power and privilege. Who has the power to identify, elevate, include, exclude, incite, or bully us? Who determines when a difference is treated as a deficit? Do you remember the cool people who condemned others to sit by themselves in the school cafeteria? Do the words of Janis Ian's classic song, "At Seventeen," ring true for "those of us with ravaged faces, lacking in the social graces," who "desperately remained at home, inventing lovers on the phone"?[17] Apart from sports or debates, why should we have to be against other groups and identities to consolidate our own? We must learn to live together with people who are different from us as well as ones who are the same.

> Identity and belonging are intertwined with power and privilege.

Learning to be and *learning to live together* aren't only about school clubs, or about whom kids hang out with in the cafeteria or the school yard. They involve the learning process too. In their award-winning book *In Search of Deeper Learning: The Quest to Remake the American High School*, Jal Mehta and Sarah Fine reported on 30 U.S. high schools they studied that broke out of the box of individual competition and relentless standardization and testing.[18] They described teachers with inspiring pedagogies, curriculum content that they had written themselves, and assessments that were tailored to their students' needs and interests.

Even in those schools, however, the critical and collaborative learning that they witnessed was mainly consigned to optional classes and extra-curricular activities. "The periphery is often more vital than the core," they wrote. This is something we need to fix—to make *learning to be* and *learning to live together* part of the whole curriculum as essential aspects of deeper learning, not just options on its periphery.

The Divided Self

The fact that our identities evolve through our relationships doesn't mean that these processes are always harmonious. Relationships can be problematic. Families can be dysfunctional. Communities can be claustrophobic. The power relationships that run through some families, schools, and societies can be oppressive and exclusionary. Instead of helping us develop and integrate our identities, they can actively constrain us. They can coerce us into hiding and dividing our inner selves, to conform to social expectations of how to be and how not to be.

If you're an educator, there's a good chance you come from a modest upbringing—a working-class family, aspiring immigrants, or parents who were also teachers. From time to time, you might find yourself thrown into an occasion that is in another social echelon altogether—a posh cocktail reception or some other elite gathering. At times like these, you might feel like a fish out of water. You do your best to fit in, to follow the ball of an unfamiliar topic in a conversation, or to fake appreciation of the baroque architecture. But you also know that you may do or say the wrong thing at any moment and give yourself away as an interloper.

If you're a spy, an actor, or even a waiter, pretending to be something that you are not is part of the job. It's a learned skill set. One reason that we are fascinated with some cinematic characters is that they excel with this kind of trickery. The 2022 miniseries *Inventing Anna* is based on the incredible true-life story of Anna Sorokin, a Russian-born con artist. Over four years, she passed herself off as a wealthy heiress in the United States. By day, Sorokin was sipping expensive champagne and wearing glamorous clothes. By night, she slept in her car to keep one step ahead of her creditors. Eventually, she went to jail for defrauding people she had connected with out of more than a quarter of a million dollars.[19]

Assuming a false identity, or engaging in identity fraud and identity theft, isn't just an issue for imposters like Anna Sorokin or the people she tricked. These issues affect many among us, in ways that are far less sensational but nonetheless bear immense significance. Consider a few everyday examples.

We must learn to live together with people who are different from us as well as ones who are the same.

What if your school, your community, or sometimes, it seems, the entire society expects you to be, and indeed presumes that you are, something you are not and don't really want to be? What if you're gay, you haven't come out yet, and your friends assume you're all in on the ribald heterosexual jokes they tell? What if you're dyslexic and you can hardly read a single word in front of you in a high-powered meeting?

Fifty years ago, Scottish psychiatrist R. D. Laing developed a theory about the causes of identity splitting.[20] Drawing on the work of Margaret Mead's third husband, Gregory Bateson, he identified adults and especially parents as being the primary cause of their young people's schizophrenic or *divided* selves. Teenagers, he said, were bombarded with contradictory, mixed messages, or "double binds," as Bateson called them.[21] "For goodness' sake, be spontaneous!" "You must *want* to do your homework!" These sorts of conflicting imperatives of how to be are impossible to fulfill simultaneously.

Laing's contentions about the parental causes of schizophrenia have not endured. But his argument that whole societies expect people to put on performances in order to conform to others' expectations still resonates. People, he said, were forced to repress their authentic, inner, true selves in favor of false selves that everyone else wanted them to be. In the language of Herbert Marcuse, they became *one-dimensional* beings.[22] They had to pursue lives of what Jean-Paul Sartre called *bad faith*.[23] It wasn't enough that they were inwardly constrained. They also had to outwardly embrace and express insincere beliefs.

What about those brave souls and free spirits who insist on pursuing their own paths in life? For critics like Laing, they were likely to end up incarcerated and lobotomized, like Randle McMurphy, the mental patient portrayed in Ken Kesey's *One Flew Over the Cuckoo's Nest*.[24] In the topsy-turvy reality portrayed by Laing and Kesey, it is the world that is mad, not those who have been institutionalized. In this analysis, false selves can't be maintained for long. Eventually they implode, as does the world around them.

Laing linked the pervasive presence of the false self to orientations toward conformity in society and in middle-class families. The false self, he wrote,

> *usually* amounts to an excess of being "good," never doing anything other than what one is told, never being "a trouble," never asserting or even betraying any counter-will of one's own. Being good is not, however, done out of any positive

desire on the individual's own part to do the things that are said by others to be good, but is a negative conformity to a standard that is the other's standard and not one's own, and is prompted by the dread of what might happen if one were to be oneself in actuality.[25]

"Being good" is an ingrained message that that has been etched into the lives and upbringing of women for centuries and that too many girls are still supposed to pick up from their teachers in school, even to this day. The focus on "being good" and maintaining institutional order is also evident in many regimes of "modern" behavior management in schools, and in "no excuses" schools in the United States with routines of strict regimentation, required silence while walking in corridors, and severe consequences, including complete isolation, for students who do not comply.[26]

These kinds of regimes and escalating steps of behavior intervention sometimes have evidence-based claims behind them that they are proven instances of "what works." But as Professor Yong Zhao of the University of Kansas points out, "what works may hurt."[27] Andy's mum (like many working-class parents at the time) used to slap him and his brothers across the back of their legs when they did something wrong, sometimes with the almost musical rhythmic accompaniment of scolding: "Don't. You. Ever. Do. That. A. Gain!" In its own way, perhaps it worked. But is slapping kids anywhere a desirable way to form human character and develop an honorable true self? That's another matter altogether.

Peers can also exert pressure on you to become someone else, and psychological sanctions can be as harmful as physical ones. You must get just the right cut of jeans, purchase the most fashionable sneakers, or acquire the perfect tattoo and body piercings. Otherwise, you're thrown into the abyss of social exclusion.

Worst of all, these days, is the constant surveillance of digital media and the prospect of being outed for the slightest deviation from the group norm. All the time, we are watched and monitored for how we are, what we do, and how we appear. As French philosopher Michel Foucault pointed out, this is a world where the possibility of doing the wrong thing or attracting criticism is anticipated by people who start to police themselves.[28] There's no need for the government to undertake disciplinary measures against you for having nonconformist ideas if you censor yourself, in advance. Nor is there any need for a school to monitor students' social media accounts if they are already afraid that one ill-tempered posting will bar them from acceptance to the top college or university of their choice.

The 21st century world of "virtual identities" can come to dominate and control even people's offline, real-world selves in other ways besides self-censorship. As well as hiding true selves, it can drive young people to flaunt idealized false ones. In a world of Instagram imagery; of Facebook, TikTok, and Twitter profiles; of self-adulating selfies; and of hours-a-day online that regularly run into double figures, it's often not even enough to be *good* anymore. You must seem to be brilliantly, beautifully, and perpetually *perfect*. When all the moments of mini-ecstasy have been posted; when all the self-portraits have been photoshopped to make the necks even thinner, the chins even sharper, and the lips even fuller; and when (in your own eyes, and those of actual and imagined peers) you still don't match up to others' fantasies of perfection, then the tangible pain of a razor blade drawn across bare skin can feel more bearable than the psychic wounds of ubiquitous disapproval.

The global mental health crisis among adolescents is due to many factors, such as poverty, economic inequality, and worries about war and climate change. However, psychology professor and social media expert Jean Twenge claims that nothing explains the growth of anxiety among girls of all social classes, and across cultures, more than their addiction to their phones.[29] Charles Cooley's *looking-glass self* has become a digital hall of mirrors for them. Supine adolescents, alone on their beds, now populate a distorting world of enhanced Instagram identities, she says. Shallow iPhone interactions, and fake Facebook "friends," viewed and posted with endless emojis, create a digital cul-de-sac of psychological bad faith.

Scapegoating digital tools for all adolescents' ills, like Twenge is inclined to do, is tempting, but also one-sided. During the worst months of the coronavirus pandemic, for example, digital tools served as a lifeline for many young people, especially those most fearful of social isolation. One survey found that more than half of young people used their social media tools to promote their mental health during the pandemic, and almost a third accessed platforms that helped them maintain inner equilibrium.[30] Digital tools helped young people continue at least some aspects of in-person relationships that the pandemic had stolen from them.

Virtual identities can also do more than sustain relationships that are no longer possible in person. They can liberate the self from negative assumptions and attributions that may be directed at it in real life.

> Nothing explains the growth of anxiety among girls of all social classes, and across cultures, more than their addiction to their phones.

When you're online, no one need know if you're old, disabled, fat, or, by the standard of prevailing norms, ugly. In many video games you can let your fantasy roam free by creating your own avatar. You can take time to become attractive to potential romantic partners without them dismissing you prematurely because of physical first impressions.

Nonetheless, alongside these identity benefits, the risks that high volumes of digital interaction pose to many young people's selves are considerable. They must be addressed in the policies and practices of schools today by limiting screen time, establishing conversations with parents about online interaction, and creating other meaningful activities that build belonging outside of digital learning. Involving students as responsible participants in these conversations is essential, too.[31]

In-person interaction in schools has not always created integrated and harmonious identities, though. Years before digital tools were even imagined, schools played a long-standing role in creating divided selves. This began with something as innocuous as teachers only asking closed questions to which they already knew the answer. The impact of this kind of stunted dialogue becomes magnified once right answers yield rewards. This could take the form of a higher mark or grade, a gold star or treat, or simply the teacher's eagerly desired approval.

In the 1960s, former U.S. submariner John Holt spent months observing classrooms. He concluded that they were dominated by a right-answer culture in which children engaged in all kinds of seemingly eccentric strategies to produce the right answer and avoid the wrong one. Most of all, they needed to stave off the impression that they had no answer at all.

Holt's best-selling books like *How Children Fail* and *How Children Learn* documented the lengths that children would go to as they tried to avoid being seen to be wrong or stupid.[32] They mumbled answers they were uncertain of. They formed their letters in an ambiguous way if they weren't confident about the exact spelling. They half-raised their hands to answer the teacher's question, so they'd be less visible and therefore less liable to be called on. And they never went back to check their work in case it was wrong. This, said Holt, is why kids don't look back. It's not because they are slapdash and don't care. It's because they are afraid of what they'll find!

The problem, Holt argued, is not that some teachers are wicked or weak. Scapegoating individuals misses the point. It's the system that's to blame—a system that is even more evident today in schools whose very existence in England or the United States can hinge on one bad inspection, or one poor set of test scores. "Our standing among other teachers, or of our school among other schools," Holt wrote, "depends on how much our students seem to know; not on how much they really know, or how effectively they can use what they know, or whether they can use it at all."[33]

This world of constant competition and of endless test preparation communicates ever-impending prospects of failure. Along with punitive behavior regimes inflicted on marginalized groups of children and ubiquitous screen-based technologies, all this teaches young people how not to be, or how to pretend to be something else. Too many schools, systems, and governments have not just accepted this world of how not to be. Demanding that children sit quietly, stay indoors, follow the curriculum, and regurgitate what they are told, schools have been actively promoting false and divided selves, far and wide.

Spoiled Identities

One of the most distressing reasons for having to project a false self is having an identity—in other people's eyes, and perhaps even one's own—that is defined by one overriding attribute that is regarded as deeply undesirable.

For all of us, at different times or in different places, parts of our identity become more salient compared to the other aspects. This might relate to our race or nationality, to our gender identity, to our movement into being parents or grandparents, or to the kind of job we have. But sometimes, we do not select the salient parts of our identity. They are imputed to or even foisted upon us, against our will. At the very least, this imputation can be irritating—as when Andy, with his British accent, is assumed by some U.S. educators to come from privilege, even though his adolescent years were spent in a low-income, single-parent household that periodically sank into poverty.

More seriously, *imputations* of one aspect of an identity that overrides all others can also lead to *amputations* of other significant parts of people's identities in ways that are inequitable, insulting, oppressive, and unjust. In *Stigma: Notes on the Management of Spoiled Identity*, one of the world's most quoted sociologists, Erving Goffman, 73rd president of the American Sociological Association, described what happens when people are treated and responded to in relation to a singular and stigmatized part of their identity.[34] Despite all the assets an individual might have, others may react to them negatively and even abusively in terms of a single "master status," as Goffman called

> Demanding that children sit quietly, stay indoors, follow the curriculum, and regurgitate what they are told, schools have been actively promoting false and divided selves, far and wide.

it, that overrides and even negates all other aspects of a person's identity.[35] So, despite all their other attributes, people are treated singularly and stigmatically as being disabled, elderly, homeless, "Native," an ex-prisoner, Asian, fat, Black, deaf, Jewish, white trash, mentally ill, or gay, to list just a few examples.

According to the ancient Greeks, a stigma is an obvious mark on a person that signals something unusual, wrong, blemished, or disgusting about them. It was common at the time to inscribe tattoos on thieves or slaves that literally branded them as having a criminal or degraded status. Goffman defines stigma in modern societies as referring to someone who possesses "an attribute that makes him different from others . . . in the extreme, a person who is quite thoroughly dangerous, bad or weak." This person is "thus reduced in our minds from a whole and usual person to a tainted, discounted one. Such an attribute is a stigma."[36] Goffman says people who are stigmatized develop "spoiled" identities that they must then manage because they are victimized, bullied, excluded, ignored, teased, pitied, patronized, and generally stereotyped in punitive and derogatory ways.

How do those who are stigmatized respond to the marks that are made upon them? Some go under. They internalize the sense of shame and isolation that online bullies, colonial powers, or racist vigilantes foist upon them. They become depressed, turn to drink or drugs, and end up in prison or among the homeless. Others follow the path described by Laing and divide themselves by creating a "false" self to increase the chances of acceptance among others—often at great cost to the inner "true" selves they are hiding. Among the self-defeating strategies that result are acting white, passing as straight, creating alternative stories to account for prison time, or talking in long monologues at parties to disguise their own deafness.

Goffman also described additional ways in which stigmatized groups manage their spoiled identities. They may band together in their own subgroups for self-help. They may organize and protest against out-groups. They can turn the characteristics that are stigmatized by others into points of pride among themselves—as with Black Power, Gay Pride, Nasty Women, and Trailer Trash. They can join new social movements forged with others who have been mistreated. On the other hand, forming subgroups in this way can also lead to fragmentation of different identity groups and to the growth of identity politics, with each group pursuing its own cause separately from or in alliance with a limited number of the rest.

In some cases, people with spoiled identities turn to violence against those they regard as their aggressors. They may also persecute other stigmatized groups, such as immigrants and refugees, or people of different faiths. Those who are bullied can end up bullying others. This is how Australian author Kate Grenville, in *The Secret River*, a fictionalized history of her own colonial ancestry, describes the racist attitudes and behavior of deported and grossly maltreated white British convicts toward the aboriginal populations they encountered.[37] Exclusion doesn't always generate responses of inclusion. Its oppressive marks can get passed on to others.

> Exclusion doesn't always generate responses of inclusion. Its oppressive marks can get passed on to others.

Erased Identities

Even worse than stigmatization of people's identities is complete suppression of them. Unwanted and oppressed identities can be targets for eradication by governmental, colonial, and institutional powers. These acts of cultural genocide begin in schools when they are used as instruments of state subjection. Placing generations of Indigenous children in state residential boarding schools where they were separated from their families and communities, prevented from speaking their own languages, denied access to their own historically rich cultures, and treated with appalling cruelty, up until as recently as the 1990s, was a result of systematic policies to erase Indigenous identities altogether. Any efforts anywhere to forbid children in an invaded or colonized country from speaking their own language are part of the same pattern.

Bad as they are, these are by no means the only instances of identity erasure that occur in schools and society right up to the present day. Goffman, who was mentored by Everett Hughes, did one of his earliest studies in a Washington, DC, mental hospital while working undercover as a physical therapist's assistant. Building on what he learned here, he made famous a concept that described this kind of institution and others like it as *total institutions*.

Total institutions impose absolute control and total surveillance over all their inmates or their equivalents in traditional mental hospitals, military barracks, monasteries, and prisons—*and* boarding schools! "A total institution," Goffman wrote, may be defined as "a place of residence and work where a large number of like-situated individuals, cut off from the wider society for an appreciable period of time, together lead an enclosed, formally administered round of life."[38]

These institutions, Goffman said, deliberately strip their inhabitants of their dignity and identities. They do this through demands for unquestioning compliance and the repeated application and constant threat of harsh punishments. Total institutions, Goffman argued, subject their inmates to what he called "degradation ceremonies."[39] These are ritualized methods devised to strip people, sometimes literally, of their identities. Military recruits who have their heads shaved, incoming prisoners forced to take showers under the gaze of others, hospital patients who have their regular clothes confiscated, or anyone being publicly mocked and harangued in front of their peers—all these procedures deprive people of their identity, dignity, and basic humanity. In view of all this, it is not surprising that a December 2022 U.S. federal court ruling that the Marine Corps cannot deny entry to Sikhs because of their unshorn beards and hair that signify their religious faith was opposed by members of the Marine Corps leadership itself.[40]

Some researchers have claimed that schools are like total institutions. They point to the regimented ways in which classes change when the bell rings, to students only being allowed outside with permission, to young people mainly having to learn what they are told to, and to the adults always being in charge. But in an age that values play in early childhood, where interdisciplinary learning and self-chosen projects are growing, and when student voice is gaining momentum, comparing schools to prisons and asylums is stretching a point. Yet almost all schools, not just the more infamous state boarding schools or residential schools, still possess at least some of the disturbing and degrading qualities that are shared by total institutions.

In February 2020, for example, the U.K. government's education minister at the time, Gavin Williamson, praised schools with strict discipline regimes that included silent walking in corridors and instant punishments for students who were slouching in their seats.[41] Schools using these procedures, he argued, got better secondary school examination results. The National Education Union responded that these strategies were "draconian" and "inhumane."[42] They led to some students spending inordinate amounts of time out of class and away from learning. These edicts of Williamson's may be consistent with the fact that in November 2022, he was investigated for bullying his staff by telling one of them to "slit their throat," and by exhibiting other menacing behaviors such as keeping a tarantula near his desk to intimidate people who had appointments to see him.[43]

As we have already seen, some U.S. charter school chains have adopted "no excuses" policies that take away young people's autonomous judgments over the smallest aspects of their manner and demeanor. In research on these schools, Joanne Golann, assistant professor of public policy and education at Vanderbilt University, concludes that students "learn to monitor themselves, hold back their opinions, and defer to authority."[44] Their most basic aspects of identity and human dignity are taken from them. However effective these schools may be in achieving higher test and examination scores, regimes of this kind impede young people's emerging sense of self and of belonging to their communities. They deny, degrade, and destroy their students' personal and cultural identities. On human rights grounds, it is time to end them.

> Regimes of this kind impede young people's emerging sense of self and of belonging to their communities.

LEARNING TO LIVE TOGETHER

Learning to be can only be achieved through *learning to live together.* How others treat us is crucial for the kinds of people we become. This chapter has confronted the fact that, in schools and society, this treatment can turn into mistreatment or even maltreatment. Too often, in our schools and the world at large, young people have had to create, express, and live as divided selves to succeed or simply survive. This has exacted enormous personal costs, in terms of identities that have become damaged and degraded, and that have ultimately imploded.

Some of the most distressing examples of these patterns have been among individuals and groups who have been marginalized and stigmatized by powerful groups and institutions who have defined them as abnormal, or even subnormal. Very often, those who have been stigmatized have been forced to live a life of unbearable shame, or to conceal their real identities, to pretend to be someone else.

In the most egregious instances, our schools and other institutions have set about wiping away all traces of young people's distinct identities. State residential schools, some boarding schools, "no excuses" schools, exclusionary language policies, and curriculum content that impugns or ignores the cultures and identities of diverse students in our classrooms all make schools too much like total institutions that deprive young people of their distinctive, complex, and animated identities for the sake of discipline, assimilation, and control.

It's time to leave behind a world and a school system where people from diverse backgrounds have their identities—their fundamental senses of who they are and of how to be—suppressed, stigmatized, and stripped away from them. Educators must not be the overpowering adults who teach young people how not to be. They must help young people learn how to be, how to belong, and how to live together.

Schools should practice inclusion, not exclusion. They should develop integrated human beings, not internally divided ones. Instead of erasing young people's identities, they should include, enhance, and elevate them, whenever they can. Schools should find ways to recognize and value diverse identities rather than putting them down or setting them against each other.

How can this be done? Our research in 10 school districts shows that schools are making progress, but also that the record is mixed. The next chapters examine what our evidence reveals.

Notes

1. Quoted in Schubert, H.-J. (Ed.). (1998). *Charles Horton Cooley on self and social organization.* University of Chicago Press, p. 164.
2. Lady Gaga. (2011). *Born this way* [Album]. Streamline.
3. Go to https://twitter.com/WomenEd.
4. Ali, S. (2018). *The self-love workbook: A life-changing guide to boost self-esteem, recognize your worth, and find genuine happiness.* Ulysses Press; Bayer, M. (2019). *Best self: Be you, only better.* HarperCollins.
5. Tali, D. (2017, December 22). *Why growing numbers are saying "yes" to themselves.* BBC. https://www.bbc.com/news/business-42415394
6. Cooley, C. H. (1902). *Human nature and the social order.* Scribner, pp. 183–184.
7. Mead, G. H. (2015). *Mind, self, and society.* University of Chicago Press. (Original work published 1934)
8. Lortie, D. C. (1975). *Schoolteacher: A sociological study.* University of Chicago; Waller, W. (1967). *The sociology of teaching.* Wiley. (Original work published 1932)
9. Hughes, C. E. (1962). Good people and dirty work. *Social Problems, 10*(10), 3–11.
10. Becker, H. S., Geer, B., Hughes, C. E., & Strauss, A. L. (1961). *Boys in white: Student culture in medical school.* University of Chicago.
11. Hughes, C. E., Hughes, H. M., & Deutscher, I. (1958). *Twenty thousand nurses tell their stories: A report on a study of nursing functions sponsored by the American Nurses' Association.* Lippincott.

12. Hughes, C. E. (1958). *Men and their work*. Free Press.

13. Hughes, C. E. (1943). *French Canada in transition*. University of Chicago.

14. Chapoulie, J.-M. (1996). Everett Hughes and the Chicago tradition. *Sociological Theory, 14*(1), 3–29.

15. Becker, H. S., Geer, B., & Hughes, C. E. (1968). *Making the grade: The academic side of college life*. Wiley.

16. Hargreaves, D. (1967). *Social relations in a secondary school*. Routledge and Kegan Paul.

17. Ian, J. (1975). At seventeen [Song]. On *Between the lines*. Columbia.

18. Mehta, J., & Fine, S. (2019). *In search of deeper learning: The quest to remake the American high school*. Harvard University Press.

19. Brownell, J., Chang, H., & Pressler, J. (Producers). (2022). *Inventing Anna* [TV series]. Netflix.

20. Laing, R. D. (1965). *The divided self: An existential study into sanity and madness*. Penguin.

21. Bateson, G. (1972). *Steps to an ecology of mind*. University of Chicago, p. 201.

22. Marcuse, H. (1964). *One-dimensional man*. Beacon Press.

23. Sartre, J.-P. (1965). *The philosophy of Jean-Paul Sartre*. Modern Library.

24. Kesey, K. (1962). *One flew over the cuckoo's nest*. Viking.

25. Laing, R. D. (1965). *The divided self: An existential study into sanity and madness*. Penguin, p. 98.

26. Golann, J. (2021). *Scripting the moves: Culture and control in a "no excuses" charter school*. Princeton University Press.

27. Zhao, Y. (2018). *What works may hurt: Side effects in education*. Teachers College Press.

28. Foucault, M. (1977). *Discipline and punish*. Vintage.

29. Twenge, J. M. (2018). *iGen: Why today's super-connected kids are growing up less rebellious, more tolerant, less happy—and completely unprepared for adulthood—and what that means for the rest of us*. Atria.

30. Anderson, M., Vogels, E. A., Perrin, A., & Rainie, L. (2022). *Connection, creativity and drama: Teen life on social media in 2022*. Pew Research Center.

31. For more on this topic, go to Hargreaves, A., & Shirley, D. (2022). *Well-being in schools: Three forces that will uplift your students in a volatile world*. ASCD, pp. 104–116; Shirley, D., & Hargreaves, A. (2021). *Five paths of student engagement: Blazing the trail to learning and success*. Solution Tree, pp. 87–107.

32. Holt, J. (1967). *How children learn*. Da Capo; Holt, J. (1982). *How children fail*. Da Capo.

33. Holt, *How children fail*, pp. 253–254.

34. Goffman, E. (1963). *Stigma: Notes on the management of spoiled identity*. Simon & Schuster.

35. The term *master status* was actually taken by Goffman from his mentor, Everett Hughes. See https://en.wikipedia.org/wiki/Master_status.

36. Goffman, *Stigma*, p. 3.

37. Greenville, K. (2018). *The secret river*. Canongate.

38. Goffman, E. (1961). *Asylums: Essays on the social situation of mental patients and other inmates*. Anchor Books, p. xiii.

39. Goffman, *Asylums*, p. 139.

40. Taylor, D. B. (2022, December 26). Court rules Sikh marine recruits can wear beards at boot camp. *The New York Times*. https://www.nytimes.com/2022/12/26/us/sikh-beard-marine-corps.html

41. Williamson, G. (2020, February 28). Everyone benefits when school children are taught to be polite, respectful, and disciplined. *The Daily Telegraph.* https://www.telegraph.co.uk/news/2020/02/28/everyone-benefits-school-children-taught-polite-respectful-disciplined/

42. Carr, J. (2020, February 28). Williamson calls for silent corridors and banned mobiles "to be the norm." *Schools Week.* https://schoolsweek.co.uk/williamson-calls-for-silent-corridors-and-banned-mobiles-to-be-the-norm/

43. Crerar, P. (2022, November 7). Senior civil servant claims Gavin Williamson told them to "slit their throat." *The Guardian.* https://www.theguardian.com/politics/2022/nov/07/senior-civil-servant-claims-gavin-williamson-told-them-slit-your-throat

44. Golann, J. W. (2015). The paradox of success at a no-excuses school. *Sociology of Education, 88*(2), 103–199, quote from p. 103.

CHAPTER 4

Including Identities

Full inclusion is about amplifying the cultural strengths of groups and communities that have been historically neglected, stigmatized, and marginalized. Inclusion is also about honestly confronting the historical, political, and cultural forces that lead to poverty, war, racism, trauma, and the oppression of Indigenous peoples.

The opposite of exclusion is not the *absence* of exclusion. It's the active *presence* of inclusion.

Identity and Inclusion

The opposite of exclusion is not the *absence* of exclusion. It's the active *presence* of inclusion. The idea of inclusion in education is emerging as a way of rethinking and expanding beyond special educational needs. It involves leaving behind the idea of special needs as a disability, medical diagnosis, specific support system, placement within or outside a classroom, or legally required intervention, in favor of accommodating all students' learning needs. Inclusion in this broader sense is a way to accommodate, engage with, and respond to students who have been marginalized, oppressed, and poorly served by the school system, because of identities that are related to race, ethnicity, language, social class, disability, and gender status.

It is ironic that it has taken many years for the term *inclusive* education to refer to all learners, regardless of their specific identities. A 2020 report by the United Nations Educational, Scientific and Cultural Organization (UNESCO), *Towards Inclusion in Education: Status, Trends and Challenges*, recognizes that "in many countries, inclusive education is still thought of as an approach to serving children with disabilities within general education settings."[1] This orientation has meant that refugee children who had suffered the horrors of war, or transgender teenagers who were subject to relentless bullying, for example, were not included under the heading of "inclusive education." Increasingly, however, UNESCO's report says, inclusion is "seen more broadly as a principle that supports and welcomes diversity among all learners."[2] Consequently, UNESCO proposes, all educators should aspire "to eliminate social exclusion that is a consequence of attitudes and responses to diversity in race, social class, ethnicity, religion, gender, sexual orientation, migrant status and ability."[3]

This broader approach to inclusion exists more in theory, research articles, report recommendations, and scattered practices than it does in concrete policies and fully implemented practices of educational systems. By looking closely at some Canadian examples, we get a glimpse of what is practically possible and, also, of what may be challenging and difficult as the inclusion agenda expands elsewhere.

Shelley Moore is an assistant professor at the University of British Columbia in Vancouver, Canada. Her sometimes moving and occasionally hilarious book, *One Without the Other*, is full of practical examples of inclusion and exclusion.[4] With philosophical depth, Moore communicates just what inclusion in education means and why it matters. Inclusion, she says, is not about dealing with kids who don't fit, at a particular time, in a particular place, or with a specialized support person. Inclusion is about understanding that we are all fascinatingly different. There aren't people who are normal and others who are abnormal, or even, in a word we have thankfully left behind, *subnormal*. There is no such thing as normal or "the other" who is not normal. In Moore's own words and book title, we need to grasp the significance of being "one without the other."

This does not mean that kids who are LGBTQ+, or who have Down syndrome, for example, shouldn't sometimes gather with others who share this same aspect of their identities, Moore argues. But it shouldn't be like this all the time, where in a world of inescapable stigma, marginalized people congregate defensively, for mutual support. Being in groups of alike people should be chosen rather than enforced, Moore continues. Even then, amid all the commonalities, other aspects of people's uniqueness and difference still need to be recognized and valued. That's why neither of us envisages ever ending up in a retirement community, made up of only other members of our generation, playing golf, wearing pastel-colored pants, and eating early bird specials at a local restaurant. We want to be with a mix of people, young and old, engaged in all kinds of activities—not in denial about our aging identities, but not imprisoned by them, either.

Figure 4.1   Shelley Moore's Graphic of Inclusion[5]

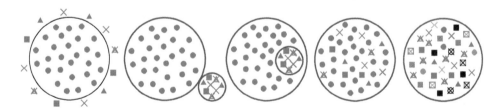

Source: Moore, S. (2016).

Moore captures what inclusion often means, and what it might truly mean, at its best, in a highly generative graphic. On the left of Figure 4.1 is a world where people with disabilities and other kinds of oppressed and marginalized identities are all outsiders—pejoratively labeled "cripples," "homos," "fatties," and a range of abusive racial epithets that are too offensive to repeat. On the right is a world where everyone can be themselves—possessing and expressing a range of identities that make them utterly unique.

In between, most educators tell us, is where their schools and systems are struggling now. Sometimes they send kids who are different to another school. More frequently, they place them with another class or group for part of the day. At times, they dedicate a support person to a student who requires extra help, or to their teacher. This assumes that most kids are normal and that the ones whose difference is a problem in some way need to be separated out as a special group. The hardest place to reach is the far right-hand side, where there's no such thing as normal at all.

Andy's ADHD, for example, should not be seen primarily as a deficit or a disorder, as the American Psychiatric Association would have it.[6] Rather, his way of being neurodiverse is an asset, in some respects, because it spurs creative thinking, capacity to improvise, ability to network, and prodigious work rate and energy. It is also a challenge when he occasionally collapses from exhaustion, forgets things that matter, and takes on too many projects. Indeed, Andy is one example of many that illustrate why we need to do away with the whole binary cataloging of assets and deficits, where traditional educators insist that underachieving students and their families have deficits, while advocates for underserved and marginalized students proclaim that we should only recognize strengths instead.

In truth, we are all a mixture of strengths and weaknesses. We need to build on people's assets but also be honest about limitations. Candidly addressing what has been causing behaviors like poor or absent parenting, or mental health problems, for example, is necessary to protect the children who are affected by them. If we can do away with other binaries, surely we can dispense with the binary of assets and deficits too.

> If we can do away with other binaries, surely we can dispense with the binary of assets and deficits too.

Intergenerational trauma among Indigenous peoples who have been subjected to cultural genocide, or among former refugees who may have experienced multiple incidences of violence, loss, displacement, and death, causes problems of anger, suicidal thoughts, and difficulty in forming relationships and expressing love. These very real difficulties should not be labeled as personal deficits, but they should not be swept aside in favor of seeing nothing but strengths, either. Full inclusion is about amplifying the cultural strengths of groups and communities that have been historically neglected, stigmatized, and marginalized, and about capitalizing on their value in the curriculum and learning that takes place in the school. Inclusion is also about honestly confronting the historical, political, and cultural forces that lead to poverty, war, racism, trauma, and the oppression of Indigenous peoples.

The Ontario Ministry of Education's 2014 report, *Achieving Excellence*, rightly recognized that schools could play major roles in identity building and in the development of well-being.[7] It embraced inclusion of identities as a central principle of achieving equity. After a "youth engagement process" that entailed "extensive youth dialogue" in "face-to-face" and "interactive workshops" throughout Ontario, along with an online survey, a 2012 report published by the Ministry of Children, Community and Social Services, *Stepping Stones: A Resource on Youth Development*, affirmed that the "sense of self" is a "core concept" and a "force of gravity" that "connects aspects of development and experience together."[8] The report noted that "for some individuals of Aboriginal descent, the sense of self has a spiritual significance."[9] Francophone youth, too, "may perceive their French heritage and language as a central component of their core self."[10] Many groups benefitted from foregrounding identity and inclusion in Ontario's educational strategy.

Through our data, we will examine the benefits that accrue when identities that were once invisible or undesirable are brought, in a positive way, to the forefront of educational attention. We don't and can't address all identities in this book, not least because not all of them are evident in our data sample. We draw on the identities that are most prominent in our evidence, and that also cast light on identity issues facing educators elsewhere. We start by looking at how educators have developed an inclusive approach to five groups of students:

- Students with special needs
- Indigenous students
- Linguistic minorities
- Students with LGBTQ+ identities
- Immigrant students

Special Needs

Educational success is hard to secure if students cannot see themselves in the school and its curriculum. There is no educational equity without inclusion of identity. Having to succeed by hiding or ignoring who we are condemns us to the tyranny of Laing's divided self.[11]

What we now think of as *inclusion* originally began as a movement to improve education for students with special needs. Within our own living memories, there was a time when societies treated those with disabilities using language that seems unbelievably repugnant and

There is no educational equity without inclusion of identity. Having to succeed by hiding or ignoring who we are condemns us to the tyranny of Laing's divided self.

inhumane today. Students and others with special needs were labeled as "cripples," "spastics," "Mongols," "backward," and "retards." People with special needs lived in the first circle of exclusionary hell.

Progress from this point occurred due to meticulous research and courageous advocacy. In the 1960s, University of Toronto professor Frank Hayden designed rigorous studies showing that children with cognitive disabilities could participate in competitive sports just as well as other children.[12] His landmark findings helped spark the first "Special Olympics" with over 1,000 participants in Chicago in 1968. This and the subsequent Special Olympics that evolved into the Paralympics were founded by President John F. Kennedy's sister, Eunice Kennedy Shriver. She was inspired to undertake this work by another sister, Rosemary Kennedy, who had intellectual disabilities. After more relentless campaigning, the U.S. Congress passed the Education for All Handicapped Children Act in 1975, which was later renamed and reauthorized in 1990 as the Individuals with Disabilities Education Act (IDEA).[13]

Meanwhile, in the United Kingdom, the Warnock Report on special educational needs was published in 1978.[14] In the ensuing Education Act of 1981, children previously described as handicapped were redefined as pupils with special needs.[15] The act required schools to give children a written statement of those needs, and the educational environment moved toward increased in-school integration.

In Ontario, in 1980, Bill 82 set out provisions for schools to educate students with a range of "exceptionalities" and established an IPRC (identification, placement, and review committee) process for every child identified as having special needs.[16]

The shift toward greater special education inclusion had global dimensions. It was enshrined in legislation but also advanced due to many kinds of civic activism. For example, in March 1990, over three dozen activists with physical disabilities, including 8-year-old Jennifer Keelan-Chaffins, put aside their wheelchairs and other mobility aids to crawl up the 83 steps of the U.S. Capitol to protest the many barriers that limited their full participation in society. The "Capitol Crawl," as it was called, is considered by historians to be the tipping point that led the U.S. Congress to pass the Americans with Disabilities Act in June 1990.[17]

In 1994, the World Conference on Special Needs Education in Salamanca, Spain, convened over 300 educators from 92 countries to promote "new thinking" on the education of students with disabilities. The ensuing *Salamanca Statement and Framework for Action on Special Needs Education* recognized that schools could be among "the most effective means of combating discriminatory attitudes, building an inclusive society, and achieving education for all."[18]

A dozen years later, however, Professors Mel Ainscow and Margarida César decried how disabilities legislation had become bureaucratic and medicalized—obsessed with classifying problems and recommending specific interventions or tiers (levels) of increasing intervention to solve them. They urged educators to consider "individual differences not as problems to be fixed, but as opportunities for enriching learning."[19] The best way that this could be done in schools, they said, would be "where there is a culture of collaboration that supports problem-solving or project work."[20]

In 2005, around the time of these wider developments, the Ontario Ministry of Education published *Education for All.* It asked district leaders to "assist teachers in helping all of Ontario's students learn, including those students whose abilities make it difficult for them to achieve their grade level expectations."[21] All districts were subsequently funded, under a new policy of *Essential for Some, Good for All,* to undertake innovations that would provide better support for students with learning challenges.[22]

INNOVATIONS THAT ARE ESSENTIAL FOR SOME AND GOOD FOR ALL

- *Universal Design for Learning* became a guiding philosophy of inclusive principles for designing curriculum and classroom learning experiences so that they fit every child.

- *Differentiated instruction* encouraged educators to understand each student's strengths and needs before deciding on the best pedagogy for them, and it stimulated schools to design strategies that would support their diverse learners.

- *Collaboration and cooperation* were, in line with Ainscow and César, recommended as effective ways to implement universal design principles.

- *Assistive technologies* were also promoted as resources that could enable teachers to differentiate their instruction effectively and enable all students to access and express their learning successfully.

One of the districts in our research exemplified how to attend to the strengths that students with disabilities possess. It created an Assistive Technology Learning Center (ATLC) to enable students with disabilities to have "great access to and success with the curriculum." Students received training and support from the ATLC in one or two 8-week cycles. They learned how to use assistive technologies like talking word processors, dictation tools, eye tracking devices, and guided reading tools. They studied the lives of highly accomplished individuals such as Keira Knightley, Anderson Cooper, and Albert Einstein who shared the students' own disabilities and could serve as role models for them.

Last, they developed skills in self-advocacy so that they would be able to articulate what they needed from their teachers and why—whether there was a quiet space away from distractions, an opportunity to move around, or an option to express their learning in a different way, for instance.

These processes empowered students to teach their peers and sometimes even their teachers about the new digital tools that could benefit everyone. What was essential for them was good for everyone. "Some of those ATLC kids are the leaders," one teacher observed. "It's the first time they've ever been able to shine. It's huge because now they're leading the whole class. That's amazing!"

The growth in students' confidence with using new technologies that their teachers adapted to fit their individual needs made it possible to create a new kind of "classroom environment that promotes the use of assistive technology as a norm and not as a dissimilarity," one educator remarked. Instead of students with special needs being the only ones using assistive technologies, digital tools became normalized for everyone—setting a trend that is now almost ubiquitous after the COVID-19 pandemic. Here, having special needs no longer bears a stigma. It is one of many indicators of difference, a source of confidence, and a spur to student leadership.

A second district assembled a Learning Disability Steering Committee comprised of teachers, special education consultants, administrators, a school psychologist and speech–language pathologist, and the director of the local chapter of the Learning Disabilities Association of Ontario to lead a transformation toward greater inclusion. The steering committee set out *if–then* statements to guide their logic model of thinking.

Members of the steering committee "went out to 10 different schools" to do interviews with "about 70 students." They were "quite taken aback" by some

STATEMENTS TO GUIDE THINKING AROUND INCLUSION

1. *If* we document how to better understand the conditions that are making successful experiences possible for students who learn differently, *then* we can mobilize knowledge regarding the interventions, strategies, and activities.

2. *If* students who learn differently are to be supported to meet their learning needs, *then* teachers need professional development and resources that have been developed collaboratively between special education and program departments in consideration of all learners.

3. *If* we provide direct instruction so that individual students have an understanding of how they learn, their learning disability, and their right to accommodations, *then* they will be effective self-advocates from junior kindergarten to school exit.

of their findings. While over 85% of students who were interviewed could label their weaknesses, few could identify their strengths. The students had internalized the deficit orientation that their schools and society had imposed upon them. They were a long way from an affirmative approach to disability and identity. Almost none of the students "actually spoke directly to asking the teacher to provide an accommodation," and no student made any mention of self-advocacy as an important part of their own individualized education program (IEP). These survey results "prompted people to think about 'Why haven't I ever included that in my own IEP?'"

This led to some frank conversations about the professional jargon and inaccessible language in which IEP statements were written. "The IEP has not been for anybody but those with a doctorate degree," one teacher said. "It's too convoluted, too complicated for the student and for the parent to understand, let alone for the teacher to input [into the online tracking system]."

Some teachers wanted a self-advocacy page in the IEP "so that it's documented, it's committed to, and it will be fully understood by the student and the teacher, because they'll develop it together." The district was moving "more toward classroom teachers being responsible for the development of IEPs for their students" "to help them speak for themselves, and to see what they need to be successful." "Even with my little guys," one teacher reflected, "I'll tell them that 'some kids are best at what they hear and what they say, and some with their eyes and with their hands. This is how you learn best.'"

Several Canadian provinces are leading the world in their more all-encompassing approach to inclusion than the traditional emphasis on special educational needs has upheld. Yet, a 2023 developmental evaluation report of Nova Scotia's Inclusive Education Policy that Andy conducted with Professor Jess Whitley and their Canadian team showed that while educators welcomed newly introduced professional learning and development opportunities on topics like antiracism, culturally responsive pedagogies, dealing with trauma, and educating African Nova Scotians, more traditional areas of special education inclusion, such as ADHD, dyslexia, and neurodiversity, seemed to be overlooked.[23]

One of the risks of trying to ensure greater inclusion for students and their identities on the grounds of language, race, ethnicity, and gender identity may be that students' identities that are associated with special educational needs get pushed into the background. Indeed, parents of students with special needs who were interviewed for the evaluation sometimes complained of feeling they constantly had to advocate for

> The students had internalized the deficit orientation that their schools and society had imposed upon them.

their children's needs, against a system that was somewhat inflexible, underresourced, and unresponsive.

Canada is on the leading edge of inclusive educational strategy. It is also the canary in its own coal mine. By digging deeper into inclusion than almost any other nation, it is ironically at risk of disproportionately marginalizing those very students and families for whom inclusion was originally intended.

Indigenous Identities

One of the first ways that Ontario expanded its approach to inclusion beyond special educational needs was in relation to educating Indigenous students. Kathleen Wynne became premier of Ontario in 2013. As a former education minister with a master's degree focused on Indigenous languages, Wynne was eager to use education to help rectify the historic and continuing injustices inflicted on the province's First Nations, Métis, and Inuit (FNMI) peoples.

There are somewhere in the range of 220 to 350 million Indigenous people around the world. The term *Indigenous* commonly refers to the original or traditional inhabitants of a region that has been settled or colonized by others who have taken control of the area, usually through frontier exploration, military conquest, and subsequent government control. Among the thousands of Indigenous groups are the Mapuché of Chile (the only group to survive the slaughter of Indigenous peoples in Chile by the Spanish conquistadores); the Hmong who are dispersed across parts of China, Vietnam, Thailand, and Laos; and the Sámi peoples who migrate across the northern territories of Norway, Sweden, Finland, and Russia.

Canada has a large and growing Indigenous population that is commonly disaggregated into three groups. First Nations peoples are bands that live south of the Arctic Circle. Métis peoples are a blend of Indigenous and non-Indigenous ancestry. The Inuit live north of the Arctic Circle. These three groups are sometimes comfortable with being referred to by the collective acronym FNMI. At other times, they prefer to be kept distinct.

Without a doubt, Canada's treatment of its Indigenous peoples is the country's national disgrace. FNMI students suffer the greatest educational inequities in Canada overall, as well as in Ontario specifically. In 2018, 47% of First Nations students, 67% of Métis students, and 59% of Inuit students graduated from Ontario's English-language high schools in four years, compared to a provincial average of 79%. In

Grade 3 reading, 53% of First Nations students, 61% of Métis students, and 48% of Inuit students reached Level 3 or 4 proficiency, compared to 72% of the whole population.

Historically, economically, and politically, the reasons for these inequities are not hard to see. Canada's Indigenous population has been subject to the same appalling injustices, indignities, and inequities of its counterparts in other parts of the world. Acts of genocide were committed against almost every Indigenous nation by European colonizers. Blankets and food were poisoned, territory was seized and stolen, and Indigenous populations were moved onto reservations, where they were forced to rely on colonial decisions for the basic necessities of life.

Many FNMI communities in Canada were forcibly removed from their land to make way for mining industries and military installations. They were relocated in desolate places, often on territory with wholly different ecosystems from those of their ancestral lands. They were stripped of any sense of time, place, and belonging. Until as late as the 1990s, children were taken from their families and placed in distant residential schools where they were deprived of their language, mistreated, and abused in the name of being civilized into Canadian culture. These were the very worst kind of Goffman's total institutions. According to the final report of the Truth and Reconciliation Commission of Canada in 2015, the government practiced "cultural genocide" against its Indigenous population, defined as "the destruction of those structures and practices that allow the group to continue as a group."[24] Colonization almost obliterated Indigenous identities.

Only in 2016, after a long, drawn-out legal battle, led by Gitxsan First Nations activist and McGill University professor Cindy Blackstock, did the Canadian Human Rights Tribunal rule that the government was systematically discriminating against 163,000 First Nations children by underfunding child welfare and support services.[25]

Then, in 2021, over 2,000 unmarked graves of children who had attended residential schools in central and western Canada were uncovered by ground-penetrating radar and other means. Although the Indigenous community had complained for decades about unrecorded deaths in the schools, it was only when irrefutable scientific evidence revealed the magnitude of the tragedy that the government was forced to acknowledge its role in concealing the deaths, along with that of Christian organizations that ran many of the schools. The government established September 30 of each year as a National Day for Truth and Reconciliation, honoring the "children who never returned home and survivors of residential schools, as well as their families and communities."[26] A compensation package was eventually agreed upon in 2022.

Suicide rates among FNMI youth are the highest in Canada. Water quality, absolute poverty, life expectancy, and infant mortality are at levels that are more typical of developing countries. Canada, one of the most prosperous economies in the world, still has intense poverty in its midst. The educational experiences of FNMI students reflect that.

Before Wynne took over the reins of government, there had already been moves to close achievement gaps in literacy and numeracy, and to improve high school graduation rates among Indigenous students. Greater collaboration was established among school districts and FNMI organizations. An FNMI advisory council was formed, along with a Directors' Council on Indigenous Education.

In 2014, the ministry launched a new implementation plan for its FNMI policy framework. This was followed by a 2015 report: *The Journey Together: Ontario's Commitment to Reconciliation With Its Indigenous Peoples.*[27] The government provided for increased funding for FNMI education, including for Native languages such as Ojibwe, Cree, and Mohawk. New Native studies programs proliferated.

FNMI histories and cultures began to be integrated into classroom learning through a rigorous treaty curriculum and a residential school curriculum. All Ontario's students, including Andy's elementary-age grandchildren, were made aware of how colonial history had affected FNMI peoples. By 2019, the number of FNMI students meeting provincial standards in mathematics, reading, and writing was increasing, along with graduation rates for Indigenous students.

Concerted efforts were now being made to support Indigenous students' well-being and to address stubborn inequalities. This was done not just by identifying gaps, raising expectations, and working harder with conventional improvement and intervention strategies, but also by enabling Indigenous students and their cultures to feel and be included in what schools offered. The implications of *Achieving Excellence* led to completely rethinking what sort of learning environments most suited FNMI young people, and what kind of curriculum content and experiences could name and address the historic injustices of residential education and its legacy. This has been the beginning of genuine inclusion of Indigenous identity in the curriculum in Ontario's schools.

One of the districts in our consortium, in the remote northwest of the province, has a large Indigenous student population. Until around 2014, it had pursued traditional improvement strategies such as data-driven interventions to raise expectations for Indigenous students and to counter deficit-based explanations for their lack of educational success. For instance, some teachers at the time believed that because many of the students had fetal alcohol spectrum disorder, not only could they not read or write, but the students were, in effect, "alingual"—without language. These teachers mainly felt their job was to care for these extremely vulnerable young people, rather than also improving their academic success.

When Premier Wynne and her minister of education, Jamaican-Canadian Mitzie Hunter, started to pursue equity by recognizing and including the identities of the province's most marginalized students, the district felt empowered to initiate some bold change strategies. Policy liberated it.

One place to start was space and design. Western schools are the product of architecture originally designed for the regimented Prussian military, the cloistered Catholic monastery, and the Victorian industrial factory. They are boxlike, linear, and closed in, with ranks of student lockers lined up in long corridors that would not look out of place in total institutions such as prisons or army barracks. The inside is walled off from the outside. Classrooms are segregated from each other. All around the globe, teachers eager to inspire students find they work in architectures that induce alienation and isolation from the outside world.

In contrast, just over two hours' drive away from the district, the University of Manitoba has built a state-of-the-art Indigenous learning center. This departs dramatically from the Western norm. Light cascades in through the roof. Indigenous symbols are everywhere. Lounging and formal meeting spaces are organized in circles and ellipses instead of the long rectangles of angular tables usually found in most offices, universities, and seats of Western government. Nobody has a seat of power. Everyone is in full view. The center provides a calm meeting place for many kinds of students, including international students of color, who also feel welcomed and supported there. What is essential for FNMI students, it turns out, is good for all.

Circles are an integral element of Indigenous cultures. Knowledge is organized in shapes like the Medicine Wheel of Learning, not in hierarchies or pyramids.[28] Indigenous practices of restorative justice take place in circles, not in a courtroom that puts the prisoner in a dock and sits the judges above everyone else. Indigenous justice doesn't only determine why a perpetrator committed a crime. It also asks how the community of which everyone is a part contributed to the act of wrongdoing. It involves discussing what actions of redemption not only the culprit, but everyone, can take that will reduce the likelihood of similar

> Indigenous justice doesn't only determine why a perpetrator committed a crime. It also asks how the community of which everyone is a part contributed to the act of wrongdoing.

wrongdoings in the future. Justice is a circular, collective responsibility, not a linear, individual one.

In the district, as at the University of Manitoba, Indigenous art and architecture are reflected in the design of school buildings. In one school, the main hallway has the seven sacred "Grandfather Teaching" symbols carved into the floor (see Figure 4.2). These are honesty, humility, wisdom, love, courage, respect, and truth. The school has created a seating area that serves as a spiritual and alternative learning space. It also has Indigenous art, including traditional animals painted on the walls and floor of the gym, as well as students' art hanging throughout the building. Students are surrounded with signs and spaces that reflect their cultural heritage and identity.

Figure 4.2   School Floor With Engraving of Seven Sacred Grandfather Teachings

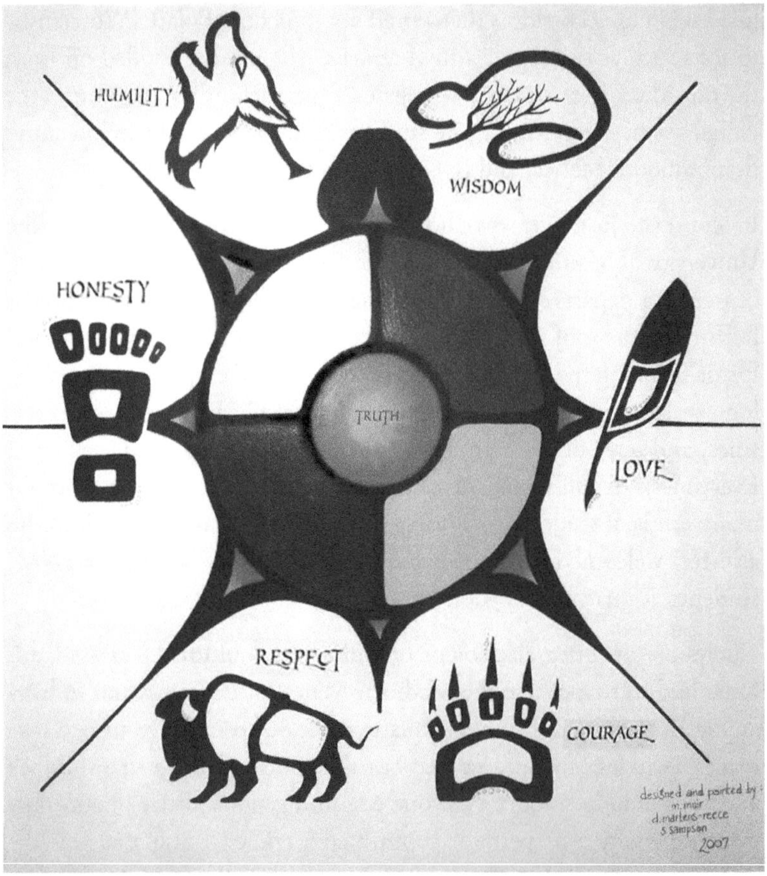

Source: Council of Ontario Directors of Education Report, 2018.

Another elementary school in the district, with an Indigenous student population exceeding 80%, built a culture room as a gathering place for families and as a space to host traditional feasts and powwows. It has a kitchen and a traditional drum. "It's fascinating to watch who gravitates to the drum," the vice principal said. "Our community drummers—it's interesting to watch the kids that will take part in the dance, and everyone sort of does their own, they have their own connection to it."

A huge part of Indigenous culture and heritage also involves learning outdoors, in what is called "land-based" learning.[29] Teachers in the district used an innovation grant to collaborate with an Indigenous caseworker to develop an outdoor education program that involved canoes, dog sledding, traditional fishing techniques, building fires and shelters, and other life skills. Building fires and shelters aren't just physical survival activities or cultural folkways. They connect Indigenous people's identity with culture and nature. This is essential for all of us in our relationship to a sustainable planet as an integral part of who we are.

Partly due to these innovations, attendance improved, and student engagement increased. An inclusive approach to Indigenous education means valuing land-based learning as much as indoor learning. It involves incorporating traditional forms of knowledge and knowledge keeping in the curriculum.

Increasingly, these ways of learning are also an important part of everyone's education. Nordic countries, for example, punctuate the school day every 50 minutes or so with a few minutes of outdoor play.[30] Outdoor play has become embedded in the early childhood curriculum in countries such as Scotland. Learning outdoors cures the "nature deficit disorder" that author and journalist Richard Louv says is affecting and afflicting children who spend too much time indoors because of test preparation and excess screen time.[31]

In a Canadian Playful Schools Network that Andy codirects with Dr. Trista Hollweck at the University of Ottawa, many of the participating schools are making innovations in outdoor or land-based learning. Sometimes these projects are designed for Indigenous students themselves. One school, located on Algonquin First Nations land, is connecting learning to traditional activities for each moon. These include deer skinning and medicine walks in November, snowshoes and cross-country skiing in January, maple syrup collecting in March, paddle making and goose hunting in April, and crafts related to birch bark materials in May. The purpose of this work is to "enjoy the land," undertake project-based learning, and get students away from spending too much time using technology as entertainment. Another school links the curriculum to the Cree calendar by integrating medicinal plants into science teaching.[32]

This does not mean Indigenous identity and learning on the land are separated from other aspects of learning in the modern world. Schools that value land-based learning are not retreating to nature. They are living and engaging with it. The school on Algonquin First Nations land also teaches computer coding, for example. Another school serving Inuit students in the Arctic is studying and testing local water quality and developing a water filtration system with the use of a 3D printer and supplying it back to the school for the students.

Nor are these projects involving "green" innovations and engagements with Indigenous knowledge and culture only for Indigenous students themselves. A school in eastern Canada believes that elements of outdoor learning will help build stronger connections with the accomplishments of the local historic African Nova Scotian community. Other schools without significant numbers of Indigenous students want to connect students to First Nations places of learning and the idea of nature as a guide for life development, or to use Indigenous pedagogies, gardening projects, and science investigations in the local river as ways of getting all students to connect with, value, and include sources of Indigenous culture and identity.

Land-based learning offers everyone a sense of awe and spirituality. It is connected to nature and sustainability. It improves emotional, cognitive, and physical well-being. What's essential for Indigenous learners is good for everyone.[33]

An inclusive approach to Indigenous identity also means having honest conversations about the cultural genocide of the residential schools. An elementary principal in our northwestern district, for example, described one lesson where Grade 7 and 8 students interviewed families to talk about how it had affected them. Students learned to conduct interviews, study local history, and engage with diverse perspectives on the residential school system. They then linked what they learned about their community's history with colonization to the youth suicide crisis on their own and other First Nations reserves. This has similarities to learning about the brutal legacy of slavery in U.S. schools.

These ways of including Indigenous issues and confronting colonial oppression were enabled by the province's new policy framework that put identity and inclusion at the forefront of the effort to improve equity. This is necessary because the sense of stigma and shame attached to Indigenous identity has been immense. Years of work by Indigenous educators have made recovery of their cultural identity central parts of their own development. Writing in the *Journal of Indigenous Social Development*, Natalie St. Denis, for example, described how she had self-identified as a white French-Canadian woman when she was growing up. This broke down when as an adult she looked in her mirror one morning and "was shocked by my reflection—an Indigenous woman was staring back at me."[34] Only then did she begin to accept her Mohawk ancestry on her father's side, and her blend of Mi'kmaq and Maliseet peoples on her mother's side. During a four-day vision quest, St. Denis's confusion over who she really was became overwhelming. She told a Cree elder, "I am nothing—I have no sense of belonging."[35] His response was comforting: "This is a good thing. You can see this part of yourself as an empty bubble and you get to decide what you put in it. It's up to you."[36]

Indigenous identity in Ontario's schools is being rekindled through connecting learning to nature and embedding it in nature, not just for Indigenous students themselves, but for all students.

Indigenous knowledge and pedagogies are seen as having value for all learners. Engaging with the historic oppression of Indigenous peoples, and with the attempts of colonizing cultures to obliterate Indigenous identity, is deepening learning and critical thinking among all students.

> Indigenous identity is being rekindled through connecting learning to nature not just for Indigenous students, but for all students.

Linguistic Identities

Language is a fundamental part of our identity. It enables us to discuss events from the distant past and to plan for a preferred future in a way that distinguishes humans from all other creatures. From the moment we pick it up at our parents' knees, language is our heritage. We *are* what we *speak*.

> We *are* what we *speak*.

Throughout history, and up to today, attempts to assimilate dissident or colonized cultures have involved efforts to eradicate their languages. Children who tried to speak their own language in school, or out on the playground, sometimes had it beaten out of them. Basque, Gaelic, Uighur, and Indigenous languages like Ojibwe and Cree, for example, have been suppressed and replaced by Spanish, English, Mandarin, and English or French, respectively.

Dennis has interviewed members of an older generation of Texans whose mouths were stuffed with balled-up newspapers by their teachers when they spoke Spanish. More recently, some U.S. states have introduced and even passed propositions (like referendums in Europe) to mandate English-only instruction in schools. Ontario educators criticized the provincial standardized tests for using grammatical structures that are different from those used by First Nations students. Language is a big part of national and cultural as well as personal identity.

Canada's modern foundation is both English and French. Enshrined in the country's 1982 *Charter of Rights and Freedoms* is a legislative commitment to being an officially bilingual, multicultural society. Section 23 of the charter states that citizens of Canada "whose first language learned and still understood is that of the English or French linguistic minority population of the province in which they reside have the right to have their children receive primary and secondary school instruction in that language in that province" where numbers are sufficient to justify public funding.[37] The government of Canada affirms that it "seeks to preserve and promote the minority, by granting minority language educational rights to minority language parents throughout Canada."[38] This guarantee "cannot be separated from a concern for the culture associated with the language. *Language is more than a mere means of communication. It is part and parcel of the identity and culture of the people speaking it*" (our emphasis).[39] These rights, the government website explains, are meant to be remedial in nature, to combat the erosion of minority cultures.

The protection and reassertion of French language rights in Ontario and across Canada is part of a worldwide movement to revive heritage languages. Wales, for example, has the policy goal, pursued through education, of having 1 million, or 20% of its people, able to speak Welsh, as well as English, by 2050.[40]

In Quebec, French is the dominant language, protected by law. In the rest of Canada, the majority language is English. French must struggle for recognition in the face of English-language dominance. French language and culture have minority status in Ontario. Members of the historic French-language community constantly battle against forces of long-standing marginalization and oppression. Comprising less than 5% of the population, Ontario's traditional francophone population is linguistically and culturally imperiled.

With coauthors Lindsay Bell, Michelle Daveluy, Mireille McLaughlin, and Hubert Noël, University of Toronto professor emeritus Monica Heller explains how there is more to the imperiled identity of francophones and francophonie (French culture) than population decline.[41] Economic globalization and social mobility, they say, has increased the demand for bilingual capabilities at the very same time that it has been eroding "united collective identity" and creating "breaches in solidarity" due to the growing "number of interests" in traditional communities where French language and culture have previously been prevalent.[42]

These contemporary struggles are deeply embedded in history. When Andy had dinner with system leaders in a francophone school district in the fall of 2022, they referred to 1912 like people in Ireland remember the Easter Rising of 1916—as if it were only yesterday. The government at that time issued a notorious Regulation 17. It stated that "French shall not be continued for the Study of English beyond Form 1" for French-speaking pupils. Children who could not understand English for the purposes of instruction should "begin the study and the use of the English language" as soon as they entered school.[43] Then, "as soon as the pupil has acquired sufficient facility in the use of the English language, he [*sic*] shall take up in that language the study of English."[44]

According to Canada's Compendium of Language Management, "in reality, this regulation's provisions barred French as a language of instruction in Ontario public schools."[45] The regulation remained in operation until 1944. According to the compendium, although this unjust and prejudicial law prevented French-language schools from operating, it also incurred national outrage because of its unfair treatment of one of the country's largest minority groups.

In response to the *Charter of Rights and Freedoms*, the government created 12 autonomous French-language public school districts in 1998. In these districts, according to University of Ottawa researchers Phyllis Dalley, Megan Cotnam-Kappel, and Alain Di Meglio, French, in most cases, "is the language spoken in all school spaces, both in school and extracurricular activities."[46] The Ontario Ministry of Education supports "identity-building" as a "key intervention area" for these districts. Through a process of *animation culturelle*, the task of each district is to "promote the students' academic achievement and cultural development by placing learning in a meaningful context where the French language and culture become relevant in the student's eyes." *Animation culturelle* "calls for planned and organized integration of culture into students' experiences and learning to actively contribute to their identity building."

Franco-Ontarian education was ahead of the rest of the province in asserting that identity was not a side issue, but central to any education for the whole child.

In many ways, Franco-Ontarian education was ahead of the rest of the province in asserting that identity was not a side issue, but central to any education for the whole child. Francophone districts have been thinking about how to engage students with identity issues since their inception. One educator stated that the purpose of education wasn't "about doing well on any one test; it is about preparing students for the francophone community. It is about knowing each of our students." Another said her school needed to be a place where children could "have room to run and slide and skip and jump." Play, identity, and joy belong together here.

Franco-Ontarians recovered their dignity and gained a sense of pride by standing apart and being different from the majority culture. As one school leader pointed out, and as a lesson for all educators everywhere, perhaps, among Franco-Ontarians, *identity was more important than achievement*. This kind of recognition has been banished from schools with high-stakes testing regimes for decades, but what was once a Franco-Ontarian exception is now on many schools' agendas.

Accommodating and including a minority language and culture hasn't been easy, though. In Ontario, educational and policy materials tend to be based on the content, assumptions, and idioms of English. As a result, educators in a francophone district we studied during the first phase of our work before 2012 felt that the Ministry of Education did not appreciate the challenges of educating their population. At that time, it required the exact same 100-minute mandated blocks of literacy units for their schools—with the identical structures of scaffolding of guided reading, reading aloud, and shared reading—that were used in the English-speaking schools.

This kind of standardization mandated by the ministry failed to acknowledge linguistic and cultural diversity. The "one size fits all" approach did not enable francophone teachers to give their students different allotments of time. "It is really difficult," one exasperated educator said. "We have to fight against a big machine."

By 2016, though, once identity and inclusion had moved to the forefront of the province's educational policies, one system administrator expressed how "we absolutely feel that the ministry supports what we're doing and in fact has given us the legal background to do what we do." The approaches of the district and the ministry now increasingly supported one another, rather than being at odds, as they used to be. Sometimes "we're getting the message from the district, so we see it as a message from the district and then, later on, we'll find out it's actually a message from the ministry," one elementary school teacher observed.

Franco-Ontarian educators have elevated identity as a priority and have raised its profile among all educators, although the struggle to preserve, protect, and further develop that identity will and must always continue.

LGBTQ+ Identities

In addition to her connections with Indigenous issues and to previously serving as minister for Aboriginal affairs, former premier Kathleen Wynne is and has been, among other things, a lesbian grandmother. This helps explain why her policies addressed bullying in schools of students who are perceived as "different."

The persecution of the LGBTQ+ community (identified in Canada as 2SLGBTQIA+) has a long and tragic history. Nazis put people they characterized as "homosexuals" in concentration camps, along with Jews, Roma peoples, trade unionists, and people with disabilities. Homosexuality was illegal and punishable by imprisonment in the United Kingdom until 1967, and in Canada until 1969. Sodomy remains a criminal offense in 13 U.S. states, and homosexuality is illegal and sometimes punishable by death, stoning, or torture in 73 countries. Conversion therapy, including electroconvulsive treatment, is still legal in 31 U.S. states. LGBTQ+ identities and practices are also outlawed or ostracized in many of the world's faith communities, including large swaths of denominations in the Abrahamic religions of Christianity, Judaism, and Islam.

In *Dignity for All: Safeguarding LGBTQ Students*, openly gay school administrator and best-selling leadership expert Peter DeWitt argues that among the many people who should read his book are school administrators and parents.[47] The "LGBTQ population," he says, "is the most marginalized" in school. Teenage years are hard enough, he points out, without "the extra element of needing to hide who you are because others will not like or love you anymore, including your family."[48] Some of the most vulnerable students during the COVID-19 pandemic were LGBTQ+ kids trapped in lockdown every day with homophobic parents.[49] In the developmental evaluation of Nova Scotia's inclusion strategy, Jess Whitley and Andy have found that schools and policy makers have been slower in addressing inclusion of LGBTQ+ students compared to other marginalized groups.[50]

LGBTQ+ youth are still stigmatized in Canadian schools. In one survey, 70% of Canadian students reported hearing "That's so gay" in school *every day* and 64% of LGBTQ+ students indicated that they "felt unsafe in school." This kind of pervasive bullying has impacted heterosexual students also, with 58% reporting "that they find homophobic comments upsetting." The same survey found that schools could take positive steps to address the bullying of LGBTQ+ students. Those students who attended schools with gay–straight alliances were "much more likely to agree that their school communities are supportive of LGBTQ+ individuals." On a separate survey, 88% of Ontario's students affirmed that students "wanting to form a Gay–Straight Alliance Club in their school should be able to do so."

However, there is increasing inclusion of LGBTQ+ identities in a growing group of countries through initiatives and legislative changes such as Gay Pride, gender–sexuality alliances, civil unions, and same-sex marriage. In the United States, for example, Title IX legislation, originally intended to forbid discrimination against girls and women in sports, has been updated to include LGBTQ+ populations in all areas of education. The Civil Rights Division of the U.S. Department of Justice and the Office for Civil Rights in the U.S. Department of Education also have online platforms in which parents or students can make complaints and launch investigations if they feel that students have been discriminated against because of their gender identity.[51]

Today, to be LGBTQ+ is not always as much a source of suffering and exclusion as it once was, at least in our own countries. LGBTQ+ relationships, marriages, and identities are welcomed in our own families as much as heterosexual ones. When Andy's grandchildren were 5 and 7 years old, an upcoming family wedding between two men was scarcely worthy of comment.

In the United States, a growing number of states are following California's lead in ensuring that positive representations of LGBTQ+ populations are included in history and social science frameworks. For over three decades, GLSEN, founded as the Gay, Lesbian and Straight Education Network, has developed easy-to-adapt curriculum materials at all grade levels, linked to state and national standards, that can be included in lessons. GLSEN also helps teachers to respond quickly and effectively to bullying of LGBTQ+ youth in their classes.[52]

Ontario's 2012 Accepting Schools Act decried all "gender-based violence and incidents based on homophobia, transphobia, and biphobia" in schools.[53] It urged educators to sponsor "activities or organizations that promote the awareness and understanding of, and respect for, people of all sexual orientations and gender identities, including organizations with the name gay–straight alliance or another name."

Beyond protecting students from ill-being caused by bullying, educators have sought to create a positive climate for LGBTQ+ students. One Ministry of Education policy maker said that "when two dads come in with the kid," it's important "that they're welcomed in the school." It isn't enough just to "make it really overt that it's OK," but it should be affirmative in the sense that "we're going to celebrate every child that comes into this school." Simply accepting LGBTQ+ identities is not sufficient. Genuine recognition and inclusion that acknowledge the persistence of discrimination against LGBTQ+ students are needed, too.

The francophone district's coordinator for safe and inclusive schools highlighted how the Accepting Schools Act was the foundation for all her work:

> It basically says it is the school's responsibility to provide
> a safe and accepting climate for learning. It's not anybody
> else's responsibility. It's really the school's responsibility.
> It actually lists some of the elements of that safe climate,
> for example things to do with gender or diversity of
> orientations . . . Because it's listed clearly in the legal
> framework, we feel that the ministry absolutely supports
> what we're doing.

LGBTQ+ issues were being addressed, albeit unevenly, in schools during the period of our research. Some of the evidence for this is reflected in a series of "animate" infographics that express annual feedback from a reference group of high school students to policy makers about the impact of policies within schools. The three infographics (Figures 4.3, 4.4, and 4.5) show that from 2013 to 2016, significantly more attention was being expressed with regard to LGBTQ+ issues in terms of creating an environment of safe and accepting schools. Students themselves wanted school system leaders to make more effort to allocate nonbinary restrooms, create gay–straight alliances, and deal with bullying.

Figure 4.3 Student Voice Feedback on Ontario Government's Education Policy Strategy, 2013–2014

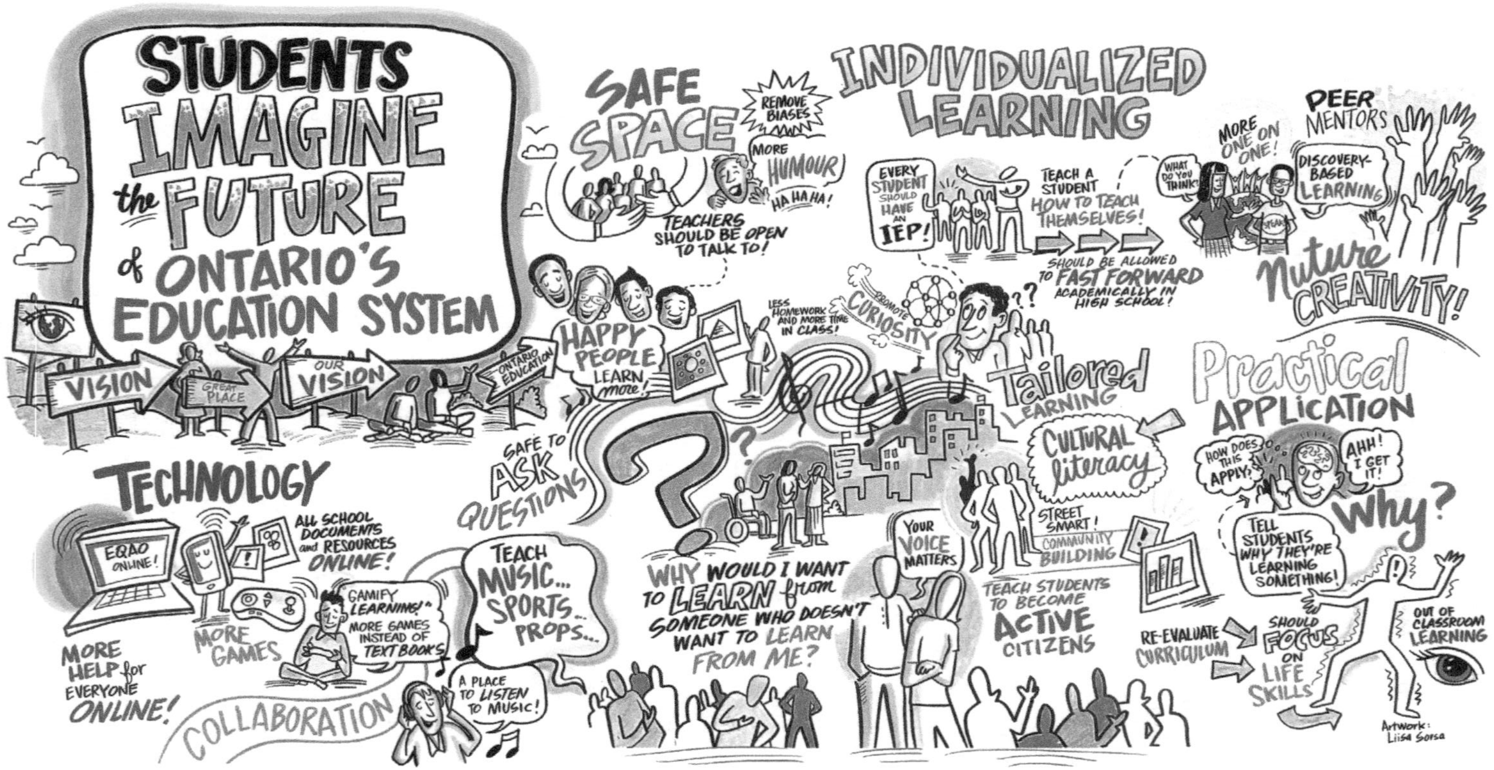

Source: © King's Printer for Ontario, 2023. Reproduced with permission.

Figure 4.4 Student Voice Feedback on Ontario Government's Education Policy Strategy, 2014–2015

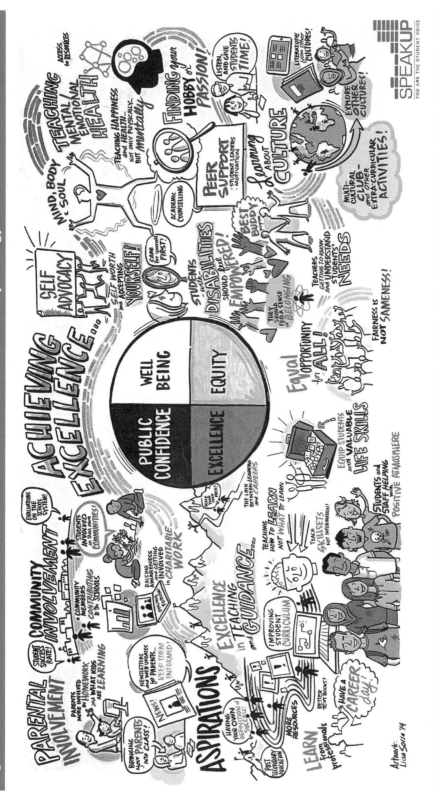

Source: © King's Printer for Ontario, 2023. Reproduced with permission.

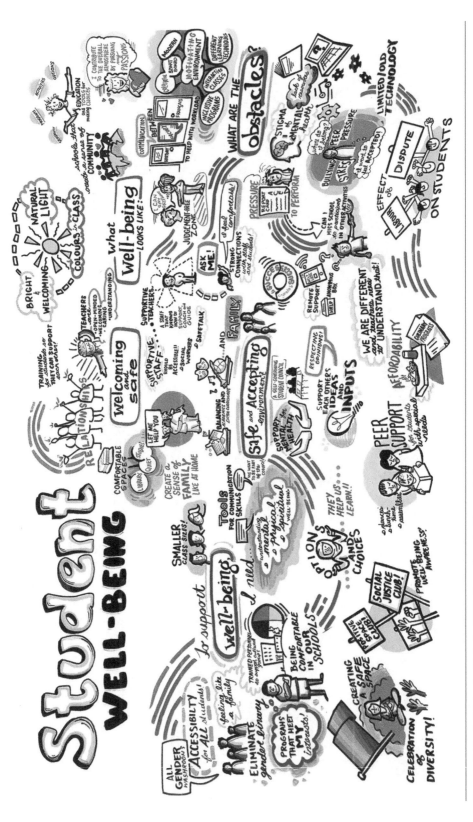

Developments that include and respond to previously stigmatized LGBTQ+ identities must be defended with constant vigilance. Equity and inclusion for LGBTQ+ students can no more be taken for granted than democracy and human rights. Homophobia remains a constant threat.

For instance, in 2018, a newly elected government stated that it would reverse a health education curriculum that had become inclusive of blended families, single-parent families, and families with LGBTQ+ parents. It proposed to revert to a 1995 curriculum that was less explicit about these issues. Widespread public outcry, however, prompted a review of this curriculum that then added new topics, such as cyberbullying. Most people felt these were improvements.[54]

This did not mean that the backlash against LGBTQ+ inclusion was over, though. In the October 2022 provincial elections, "scores" of school board trustee candidates ran on platforms that were opposed to inclusive sex education and that were antitransgender—a pattern that was repeated in other provinces and that Canada's CBC News reported as efforts to "undo policies aimed at addressing systemic discrimination."[55] In some cases, candidates were offered training by "U.S. political operatives." Candidates adopted strategies such as publicly stating that nonbinary identities are a disorder, labeling gender-affirming surgery as child abuse, and spreading conspiracy theories including a false claim that "teachers are placing cat litter in classrooms for students who identify as cats."

Valuing and including LGBTQ+ identities is by no means a completed project. Despite considerable progress in Canada, bullying and harassment persist. Political opposition continues. Catholic schools and school districts have been slower to change than other districts, as we shall see in Chapter 6.

When we create a safe, rich, and inclusive environment for LGBTQ+ students, this improves safety and inclusion for everyone. Inclusion of one group needn't arouse indignation in others. It can be something from which all students benefit.

Immigrant Identities

"Imagine there's no countries. It isn't hard to do."[56]

John Lennon's inspiring and uplifting words from "Imagine" express hope for a world without genocide, jingoism, xenophobia, imperial conquest, or separatist sentiment. In philosophical terms, the sentiment is admirable. In practical terms, however, it's useless and wrong.

Equity and inclusion for LGBTQ+ students can no more be taken for granted than democracy and human rights.

When we create a safe, rich, and inclusive environment for LGBTQ+ students, this improves safety and inclusion for everyone.

Different nations promote attachments to different cultures and languages, which can enrich all of us. Indigenous First Nations are indeed nations. Even the most ardent supporters of the United Nations acknowledge that the idea of a centralized world government could create more problems than it would solve because minority groups and smaller countries might find it harder to be heard or have their specific needs addressed. Much of the support for Brexit in the United Kingdom was driven by the sense that an abstract and bureaucratic authority in Brussels had usurped matters that properly belonged to the British people. In a world without borders, there is nobody immediately at hand to provide legal protection for people's human rights. Without participation and representation, it is impossible to be true citizens in any sense of the word at all.

Countries and their borders matter, and so do national identities. When people travel, one of the first things other people ask them is where they are from. In any sport, most of us like to watch a good game, but we are more likely to tune in to or turn up for one involving our own nation, or our hometown team. We identify with the landscape, literatures, histories, politics, and cultures of our countries of origin. We shouldn't assign moral superiority to these attachments, and we shouldn't be dismissive of or derogatory about other cultures and identities, of course. But there's a reason why the *Finding Your Roots* TV series is so popular. Where we live and where we come from help define us. These things are nourished by some of our earliest childhood memories. We grasp that our nations are not perfect, of course, but all it takes is for an outsider to criticize our country, and we feel a sense of defensiveness that comes from years of identification with an entity that is larger than ourselves.

Nations are historically arbitrary. They are mythical rather than natural constructions. They are imagined communities. Many Brexit supporters may have been insistent about the essential Britishness that was being lost in or stolen by the European Union, but, actually, British identity is a modern amalgam of four separate nations that have devolved powers, as well as an historical product of Celtic, Saxon, Viking, Roman, French (Norman), and many other kinds of ancestry—not to mention generations of more recent immigrations from the Jewish diaspora, French Huguenots, South Asia, Eastern Europe, the Caribbean, other parts of the British Commonwealth, and conflict zones around the world. British identity is a myth, albeit a powerful one.

Other countries are similarly complex. When we gave a presentation in the Kingdom of Morocco, we were warned not to show any maps of the country, because the location of its southern border is disputed by a separatist movement supported by Algeria and Libya.

Of course, it's right to fear extreme nationalism as a source of conflict and xenophobia. Nationalism can be mobilized to oppose immigration, keep out foreigners, and oppress those who are euphemistically described as "guest workers." Yet most nations are defined not just by their age-old family legacies but also by their immigrant heritages.

Skillful leaders know how to bring diverse populations together through rituals of identification that allow people to feel part of something bigger than themselves. At its best, the United States fashioned itself as a country that welcomed immigrants from around the world. Dennis remembers his mother reciting Emma Lazarus's poem "The New Colossus" with tears in her eyes:

> *Give me your tired, your poor*
> *Your huddled masses yearning to breathe free*
> *The wretched refuse of your teeming shore.*[57]

These words had special meaning for her, as her own mother had found refuge as an Irish-born orphan in Buffalo, New York, where the city's public schools gave her the first and only exposure to formal education she would ever have. Canada regards itself as less of a melting pot and more of a mosaic of composite identities but still instills collective national pride in its citizens.

Nationalism and patriotism are neither inherently good nor bad, provided they are not driven to extremes of exclusion. The war in Ukraine demonstrates there are moments in a nation's history when attachment to one's country is not only a legitimate source of belonging but also indispensable for survival in the face of invasion and occupation by a far greater military power. This has also been a key part of the identity of the island nation of Singapore, created by its founder, Prime Minister Lee Kuan Yew, as an integration of Chinese, Indian, and Malay cultures. In Singapore, each student learns a heritage language to sustain these age-old cultures, as well as English, so they can participate in the contemporary global economy in which Singapore has become spectacularly successful.

One of the most controversial aspects of immigration is a country's policies regarding refugees. According to the Global Refugee Forum, in 2018, Canada settled 28,000 refugees, for the first time surpassing the United States.[58] After Brexit, the United Kingdom put a stop to the free movement of people across its borders from other European countries and tightened up restrictions on all immigration even before the COVID-19 pandemic. In 2022, the U.K. government organized a scheme to relocate asylum seekers from the United Kingdom to Rwanda, a country that ranks very low on international metrics of human rights.[59] Note also that the very term *asylum seekers* repositions refugees as *people seeking to* enter a country and move among its settled population, rather than as *people fleeing from* violence or persecution elsewhere.

Even in Canada, when refugees arrive, it is all too easy, as the late Zygmunt Bauman put it, to "feel uneasy and afraid at the sight of homeless newcomers" and their "all too visible, destitute, woeful and powerless plight."[60] But, in his article "The Migration Panic and Its (Mis)uses," Bauman insisted that "humanity is in crisis—and there is no exit from the crisis other than solidarity of humans."[61]

When whole groups of refugee students arrive in their new host countries at the start of new school years, educators don't only have to compensate for lost schooling, offer language instruction, respond to children's post-traumatic stresses, and strengthen special educational needs provision. They also need to recognize their students' newcomer identities and to integrate them with the lives of other students, their schools, and the broader societies in which they are starting their new lives.

This is not simply a question of assimilation into the existing society. It is also an opportunity for cultural renewal and social transformation.

Students in one high school in our study were disturbed by the enormity of the Syrian refugee crisis. They responded by developing a fundraising drive to bring a refugee family to their region. "This very much came from the students," said the district's director. The students learned how to work with faith-based charities and government agencies to raise the money to turn their aspirations into reality. A family of seven from Syria arrived in October 2016 and settled successfully into their new home.

A second-grade teacher in another school asked a 7-year-old refugee from Syria to teach a "word of the day" in Arabic to his classmates. The surprising result was that the class asked if they could do five words in Arabic the next day. The student was "excited that someone cared" about an aspect of his identity that he had not been able to share before.

There is much more to including newcomer identities than these brief examples suggest, as we will see in the next chapter. But a good starting point is to understand that newcomers everywhere, in a school, a town, or a country, need to be welcomed and feel wanted and included. This can be heartening for the newcomers. It can also be uplifting for those who welcome them.

ESSENTIAL FOR SOME, GOOD FOR ALL

Identity is about who we really are. We cannot learn, teach, or lead effectively if we are constantly hiding or denying who we are, and if who we are and what we have been part of is regarded as a source of stigmatization and shame. Whether we are considering Indigenous identities or identities of disability, whether we are addressing identities grounded in language, sexuality, or immigration, our challenge in everything we do in our schools is to engage with those identities, be responsive to them, and enable them to become sources of individual and collective pride rather than suppression and shame. There can be no equity without inclusion, and there can be no inclusion without acknowledging and recognizing our students' identities. These processes and acts of inclusion don't just benefit the newly included. They benefit everyone.

> We cannot learn, teach, or lead effectively if we are constantly hiding or denying who we are.

All students, not just those with special educational needs, will be more successful when every student is involved in developing and writing their own personalized learning plan or pathway, when they have the skills and opportunity to advocate for the supports and approaches that help them learn best, and when they can and do use digital technologies to access, express, and enhance what they know.

All students, not just those of Indigenous heritage, will benefit from learning outdoors, sustainably, in nature; from being in classrooms that are not constructed like metal or concrete boxes; and from storytelling and the arts becoming a more explicit part of the curriculum.

All students, not just those who speak a minority language or come from a minoritized culture, will prosper when their identities and who they will develop into as human beings are accorded as much priority as gains and outcomes in measured student achievement.

All students, not just those with LGBTQ+ or other identities that make them all-too-likely targets for bullying, will flourish in a school environment from which bullying and stigmatization have been excised, and that becomes a safe environment in which they can thrive as a result.

All students will also benefit from welcoming and engaging with students from other cultures and with other identities. They will be all the better for having their minds expanded and their eyes opened, and from feeling welcomed themselves, just like someone from another country or culture, when they too change classes, schools, or the towns and cities where their parents or other caregivers choose to live.

This is the immense promise of identity and inclusion, not just for those who have been traditionally excluded, but for everyone, whatever their identity. It is a challenge that cannot be taken on lightly, though. Engaging fully with everyone's identity is no simple task, especially in a world where most people have multiple identities that intersect and overlap. This is the subject of our next two chapters.

Notes

1. UNESCO. (2022). *Towards inclusion in education: Status, trends and challenges.* Author, p. 23.
2. Ibid.
3. Ibid., p. 24.
4. Moore, S. (2016). *One without the other: Stories of unity through diversity and inclusion.* Portage & Main Press.
5. Ibid.
6. American Psychiatric Association. (2022). *What is ADHD?* https://www.psychiatry.org/patients-families/adhd/what-is-adhd
7. Ontario Ministry of Education. (2014). *Achieving excellence: A renewed vision for education in Ontario.* Queen's Printer for Ontario.
8. Ontario Ministry of Children, Community and Social Services. (2012). *Stepping stones: A resource on youth development.* Queen's Printer for Ontario, p. 14.
9. Ibid., p. 17.
10. Ibid., p. 19.
11. Laing, R. D. (1965). *The divided self: An existential study into sanity and madness.* Penguin.
12. Hayden, F. J. (1964). *Physical fitness for the mentally retarded: A manual for teachers and parents.* Metropolitan Toronto Association for Retarded Children.
13. U.S. Department of Education. (2023, January 11). *A history of the Individuals with Disabilities Education Act.* https://sites.ed.gov/idea/IDEA-History
14. Warnock, M. (Ed.). (1978). *Report of the committee on enquiry into the education of handicapped children and young people.* Her Majesty's Stationary Office.
15. Her Majesty's Government. (1981). *Education act.* Her Majesty's Stationary Office. http://www.educationengland.org.uk/documents/acts/1981-education-act.html
16. Ontario Ministry of Education. (1980). *A guide to Bill 82: A bill on special education.* Queen's Printer for Ontario.

17. Ginsburg, F., & Rapp, R. (2018). Making accessible futures: From the Capitol Crawl to #cripthevote. *Cardoza Law Review, 39*, 699–718.

18. UNESCO. (1994). *The Salamanca statement and framework for action on special needs education.* Author, p. ix.

19. Ainscow, M., & César, M. (2006). Inclusive education ten years after Salamanca: Setting the agenda. *European Journal of Psychology of Education, 21*(3), 231–238, quote from p. 233.

20. Ibid.

21. Ontario Ministry of Education. (2005). *Education for all.* Queen's Printer for Ontario, p. 3.

22. Hargreaves, A., & Braun, H. (2011). *Leading for all: A research report on the development, design, implementation and impact of Ontario's "Essential for Some, Good for All" initiative.* Council of Ontario Directors of Education.

23. Whitley, J., Hargreaves, A., Leslie, L., Collins, A., & Arsenault, A. (2023). *Interim report II: Developmental evaluation of the implementation of the Nova Scotia inclusive education policy.* University of Ottawa.

24. Truth and Reconciliation Commission of Canada. (2015). *Honouring the truth, reconciling for the future: The final report of the Truth and Reconciliation Commission of Canada.* Author, p. 1.

25. Blackstock, C. (2016). The complainant: The Canadian human rights case on First Nations child welfare. *McGill Law Journal, 62*(2), 285–328.

26. Government of Canada. (2023, January 30). *National day for truth and reconciliation.* https://www.canada.ca/en/canadian-heritage/campaigns/national-day-truth-reconciliation.html

27. Government of Ontario. (2015). *The journey together: Ontario's commitment to reconciliation with its Indigenous peoples.* Queen's Printer for Ontario.

28. Callahan, K. L., & Aragon, D. L. (2010). *The path of the medicine wheel: A guide to the sacred circle.* Trafford.

29. UNESCO Canadian Commission. (2021, June 21). *Land as teacher: Understanding Indigenous land-based education.* https://en.ccunesco.ca/idealab/indigenous-land-based-education

30. Sahlberg, P., & Doyle, W. (2019). *Let our children play: How more play will save our schools and help children thrive.* Oxford University Press.

31. Louv, R. (2008). *Last child in the woods: Saving our children from nature-deficit disorder.* Algonquin.

32. See www.playjouer.ca for more details about all 41 schools in this network.

33. For more details on the value of learning in nature for student well-being and development, see Hargreaves, A., & Shirley, D. (2022). *Well-being in schools: Three forces that will uplift your students in a volatile world.* ASCD.

34. St. Denis, N., & Walsh, C. (2016). Reclaiming my Indigenous identity and the emergent warrior: An autoethnography. *Journal of Indigenous Social Development, 5*(1), 1–17, quote from p. 3.

35. Ibid., p. 8.

36. Ibid.

37. Government of Canada. (2022, December 13). *Canadian charter of rights and freedoms.* https://www.canada.ca/en/canadian-heritage/services/how-rights-protected/guide-canadian-charter-rights-freedoms.html

38. Ibid.

39. Ibid.

40. Lewis, B. (2023, March 27). *Welsh: Law to help all Wales pupils speak confidently by 2050.* BBC. https://www.bbc.com/news/uk-wales-65082197

41. Heller, M., Bell, L. A., Daveluy, M., McLaughlin, M., & Noël, H. (2015). *Sustaining the nation: The making and moving of language and nation.* Oxford University Press.

42. Ibid.

43. Compendium of Language Management in Canada. (1913). *Regulation 17: Circular of instruction no. 17 for Ontario separate schools for the school year 1912– 1913.* https://www.uottawa.ca/clmc/regulation-17-circular-instruction-no-17-ontario-separate-schools-school-year-1912-1913

44. Ibid.

45. Ibid.

46. Dalley, P., Cotnam-Kappel, M., & Di Meglio, A. (2014). *Éducation comparée en contexte français et canadien. Les cas d'enseignement dans une langue minorée: Le corse en France et le français en Ontario. Faire société dans un cadre pluriculturel. L'école peut-elle didactiser la pluralité culturelle et linguistique des sociétés modernes.* Éditions Lambert-Lucas, pp. 83–94.

47. DeWitt, P. (2012). *Dignity for all: Safeguarding LGBTQ students.* Corwin.

48. Ibid., p. 3.

49. Hunte, B. (2020, March 26). *Coronavirus: "I'm stuck in isolation with my homophobic parents."* BBC. https://www.bbc.com/news/uk-52039832

50. Whitley et al., *Interim report II.*

51. For the Civil Rights Division of the U.S. Department of Justice, go to https://civilrights.justice.gov/. For the Office for Civil Rights in the U.S. Department of Education, go to https://www2.ed.gov/about/offices/list/ocr/docs/howto.html.

52. For the GLSEN curriculum standards, go to https://www.glsen.org/activity/inclusive-curricular-standards. For guidelines for teachers on how to respond to anti-LGBTQ+ bullying, go to https://www.glsen.org/activity/inclusive-curricular-standards.

53. Legislative Assembly of Ontario. (2012). *Bill 13, accepting schools act.* https://www.ola.org/en/legislative-business/bills/parliament-40/session-1/bill-13#:~:text=include%20the%20following%3A-,1.,on%20homophobia%2C%20transphobia%20or%20biphobia

54. BBC. (2018, July 12). *Canada province cancels new sex-edu curriculum after protests.* https://www.bbc.com/news/world-us-canada-44812833

55. Montpetit, J., & Ward, L. (2022, October 24). *Scores of anti-trans candidates running in Ontario school board elections.* CBC. https://www.cbc.ca/news/canada/ontario-school-board-trustee-investigation-1.6622705

56. Lennon, J. (1971). Imagine [Song]. On *Imagine.* Apple.

57. Lazarus, E. (2005). *Emma Lazarus: Selected poems.* Library of America, p. 58. (Original work published 1883)

58. BBC. (2019, June 19). *Canada resettled more refugees than any other country in 2018.* https://www.bbc.com/news/world-us-canada-48696974

59. Rwanda receives a ranking of 21 out of 100 on the metrics used by Freedom House. (2021). *Freedom in the world report.* https://freedomhouse.org/country/rwanda/freedom-world/2021

60. Baumann, Z. (2010). *Strangers at our door.* Polity Press, p. 10.

61. Bauman, Z. (2015, December 17). The migration panic and its mis(uses). *Social Europe.* https://www.socialeurope.eu/migration-panic-misuses

CHAPTER 5

Multiple Identities

"These days I live in three worlds: my dreams, and the experiences of my new life, which trigger memories from the past."

—From *A Long Way Gone: Memoirs of a Boy Soldier* by Ishmael Beah (2007)

Selves don't exist within us, as if they are timeless spiritual souls. They are human constructions, products of how societies evolve and change.

The Complexity of Identity

Ishmael Beah is a best-selling author and human rights activist. As a teenager in Sierra Leone, he was conscripted into the government army at the height of a civil war and killed people in cold blood. In *A Long Way Gone: Memoirs of a Boy Soldier*, Beah describes his horrendous experiences.[1]

When he was a child, he had to leave his village, he lost most of his immediate family, and he witnessed murders, beatings, severed limbs, and other brutal acts of violence. He walked hundreds of miles, facing near starvation, as he sought sanctuary. After he was forcibly recruited as a child soldier in the early 1990s, he was given an AK-47 rifle. His army superiors dosed him up with narcotics to stimulate aggression. Beah did not only kill his enemies in battle. He also executed prisoners and burned down villages under the orders of his commanders. Eventually, he was rescued by UNICEF, the United Nations Children's Fund, and taken to a rehabilitation center.

In 1996, Beah addressed the UN in New York City about the plight of child soldiers. In his late teens, he was adopted by a U.S. family and eventually attended the prestigious United Nations International School in New York, along with children of diplomats from around the world. It's hard to imagine, when you have dinner with Ishmael Beah, as Andy did several years ago, that all this is now part of who he is.

There's a lot more to Beah than meets the eye. He is Black. He suffered immense post-traumatic stress. He grew up in West Africa. These are the most obvious things about him, perhaps.

But Beah also loves Shakespeare. He recited soliloquies and monologues to his village elders from the age of 7. He bonded with his lieutenant commander as they went into battle together by quoting a line from *Julius Caesar* about how "cowards die many times before their deaths." Beah also had a long-standing passion for the colonial import of soccer. This enabled him, on occasions, to disengage from the surrounding climate of misery and fear. At the same time, a Walkman and cassette tapes of early U.S. rap music impressed the 12-year-old Beah with how "Black men" could speak English so fast. Later, through the care of a UNICEF nurse, along with renewing his fascination with rap music with another Walkman, Beah connected to the wider world and back to his prewar, more innocent childhood self in the rehabilitation center.

When he started his education in the United States, his public high school failed to acknowledge or engage with any aspect of this immense cultural experience. But Beah was at least able to reactivate his love of language and classics. The institution of public schooling that is often presented by liberal intellectuals as a tool of classist, capitalist, and colonial oppression was something that Beah just couldn't get enough of. He studied voraciously and won a scholarship to Oberlin College, where he majored in political science. Indeed, when Canadian Stephen Lewis, former UN Special Envoy for HIV/AIDS in Africa, visited children who were victims of war, rape, and punitive amputations, the one thing they most desperately wanted, he said, was to be able to go to school.[2]

Student identities are complex. So, therefore, is achieving curriculum relevance and cultural responsiveness. Identities cannot be checked off as pregiven categories against students' ethnocultural origins. If the likes of Ishmael Beah come into your school, being Black, a refugee from Africa, and a victim of trauma might be the first things that trigger efforts at cultural responsiveness. But Shakespeare, soccer, and rap were all ways to engage Beah too. They were indelible aspects of who he was. Finding ways to engage students and the many sides of their identities is not always immediately evident. Teachers must get to know their students as whole persons and unique individuals. They also need to avoid oversimplifying what identities are in general, including their own.

So far, we have argued that people's selves and identities are not things that are fixed inside us. They evolve and develop over time. Most social theorists now regard the self not as an object, but as a continuous and active work in process—always developing, constantly changing.[3]

We have explained that our identities don't simply burst out from deep inside us, like eruptions of our souls. Of course, there may be previously stigmatized parts of people's selves, like their sexuality or Indigeneity, that social pressures have made them feel have had to be kept hidden and that are only now able to "come out." But even then, it's not all their identities that are "coming out." It's just one aspect, albeit an important one.

Identities are also formed through our relationships with others. Some feminist writers now claim that, in a way, selves and identities exist between rather than within us. They are embedded in our past, present, and imagined future relationships.[4]

Just as selves and identities are not simple, they are not singular either. None of us are one thing—Black, or middle class, or a woman, for example. We are not solely a parent, a partner, a colleague, or a social media influencer. We can be all these things at the same time. Reducing people to one aspect of their identity, for whatever reason, good or bad,

> People's selves and identities are not things that are fixed inside us. They evolve and develop over time.

risks replaying the danger that Erving Goffman described, of positioning people and sometimes stigmatizing or stereotyping them in relation to one overriding "master status."

Our identities and our selves are complex, not simple. This is important to grasp philosophically and psychologically. It matters for every teacher in practical terms, too. All classes of students are diverse, even if that is not immediately visible. All identities are complex. But they need not be mysterious or ineffable. It is possible to understand the nature of this complexity, in general terms and in relation to every young person we teach, and to use that understanding to guide how we perceive and respond to student diversity, everywhere. Identity politics needn't divide us. It's time for all of us, as the saying goes, to pull ourselves together.

Multiple Personalities

Not long ago and perhaps even today, in popular culture and in the field of psychiatry, if we said someone had multiple personalities, this would be indicative of a psychiatric disorder. The Incredible Hulk; the compassionate Dr. Jekyll and his sadistic alter ego, Mr. Hyde; Anthony Perkins's mild-mannered hotel manager who turned out to be an evil killer in the movie *Psycho*—all illustrate this point.

The American Psychiatric Association describes dissociative identity disorder (previously known as multiple personality disorder) as "two or more distinct identities (or 'personality states')" that "cause significant distress or problems."[5] Here, multiple identity is a pathological or psychologically exceptional state that probably requires psychiatric intervention. But the idea of multiple identities and selves, or multiple presentations of the self, has a much more mundane, everyday, and practically useful meaning than this. This brings us back to the Canadian American Erving Goffman.

Identities and Impression Management

Goffman spent a lot of his time pretending to be someone else. His method of research, known as ethnography, involved undercover observation that enabled him to participate in what he was studying without being outed as a researcher—something that would be hard to get past any research ethics committee these days. Goffman was also a card shark and a card counter. He was banned from Las Vegas casinos. So, when he decided he wanted to study gambling behavior, he covertly got himself a job as a croupier. Like several other former presidents of the American Sociological Association, he also had a file kept on him by the FBI![6]

Reducing people to one aspect of their identity risks positioning people and sometimes stigmatizing or stereotyping them in relation to one overriding "master status."

It's perhaps not surprising, then, that Goffman had a strong intellectual interest in how people managed the impressions that they conveyed to others to send out signals about their preferred inner selves.

In his 1959 book, *The Presentation of Self in Everyday Life*—the most cited of his many works—Goffman described how people's identities were deliberate and variable constructions.[7] The self was not something solid and consistent inside of people, but the result of multiple presentations to different audiences. We all know that first impressions are important in an interview or on a date. However, Goffman pointed out, we manage our impressions all the time, and not just in high-pressure events. He quoted a teacher who pointed out that the best way to manage a class of rebellious youngsters is "to start off tough, then you can ease up as you go along."[8]

In a way, life is all an act. Shakespeare's Macbeth gives this insight a depressing twist on the whole of human existence when he reflects that

> *Life's but a walking shadow, a poor player*
> *That struts and frets his hour upon the stage.*[9]

Yet, even if life is all a drama, it's still not a one-act play. It's made up of different acts in different situations. Goffman cited 19th-century Harvard University philosopher and psychologist William James: "Many a youth who is demure enough before his parents and teachers, swears and swaggers like a pirate among his 'tough' young friends."[10]

There are different parts to our identities, and we draw on them in various ways. One of the most striking contrasts is between what Goffman called the "frontstage" and "backstage" of work and life.[11] This is the difference between a solicitous waiter interacting politely with a diner and the same waiter telling jokes back in the kitchen at the customer's expense. The difference between frontstage and backstage is the contrast between being calm and controlled with a misbehaving student in the classroom and being full of hilarity and profanity when later describing what went on to other teachers in the faculty lounge. Goffman explains that

> the backstage language consists of reciprocal first-naming,
> co-operative decision-making, profanity, open sexual remarks,
> elaborate griping, smoking, rough informal dress, "sloppy"
> sitting and standing posture, use of dialect or sub-standard
> speech, mumbling and shouting, playful aggressivity and
> "kidding" . . . minor physical self-involvements such as

humming, whistling, chewing, nibbling, belching, and flatulence.[12]

Managing the boundary between proper frontstage behavior and informal backstage horsing around is essential in the management of identity. When a teacher walks in unexpectedly on students' backstage antics, it's important not to get too censorious about their misbehavior, like using bad language, as if it was intended for the frontstage. Sometimes it might even be best to act as if this behavior has not been noticed at all.

More deeply than this, when students have different identities in their schools and their communities, it can sometimes be distressing or embarrassing for them when those identities collide. This is especially true if the official or formal expectations of school life are at odds with the culture and community in which a student lives. Perhaps high school students especially want to separate the home from the school to some degree, and not have their teachers and parents share everything they know about their adolescent lives. The self should not be completely borderless. Privacy still matters for all of us.

Few of us have a single way of being that transcends time and place. We are different with our family, our workmates, and our friends. We are not the same online compared to offline; in fact, a person who is opinionated and aggressive online often turns out to be shy and reserved in person.

In a world that is driving us to separate out, perseverate about, or quarrel and fight over singular, master-status aspects of our students' identities related to their gender status, race, or ethnicity, it's important to bear in mind that all of us are more complex than we seem at any one moment, or than we present ourselves to be in the company of one individual (teacher or otherwise) compared to another. This can help us to acknowledge and appreciate composite or multiple facets of our students' identities that cut across many aspects of their experiences. Let's probe more deeply into these issues by looking in detail at three kinds of multiple identities: ones that are transnational, mixed heritage, and cross-class.

Transnational Identities

University of Texas professor Angela Valenzuela grew up in the Mexican American community of San Angelo, Texas. When she was in seventh grade, she sought protection from a bigger, more confident classmate, Norma. For no apparent reason, Norma began bullying a

> When students have different identities in their schools and their communities, it can sometimes be distressing or embarrassing for them when those identities collide.

new immigrant. She put her down as one of those "Mexicans from ol' Mexico," derided her clothes, and mocked her limited English abilities. It escalated in a fight between the two girls, when Norma gave the new girl a black eye and ripped off her shirt, exposing her before her classmates in only her bra.

Valenzuela was "deeply ashamed" of her passive reaction to this altercation, "as if I had done something wrong."[13] Years later, while studying the sociology of education at Stanford University, she learned that these experiences can lead to forms of "internalized oppression" in which "minority group members subscribe to the dominant group's negative stereotypes of their group."[14] The curriculum mandated by the Texas Education Agency taught Mexican American youth that ever since the Mexican–American War of the 1840s, they were "losers and that Anglos were culturally and militarily superior."[15] Excessive and exclusionary nationalism in curriculum materials inflicts harmful cultural stereotypes so that, as Valenzuela says, minority students experience "soul wounds."[16]

What's the alternative? Valenzuela's University of Texas colleague, Professor Allison Skerrett, is a Caribbean immigrant to the United States. She has devoted much of her career to researching what she calls *transnational identities.* These are immigrant students' identities that can connect or collide when their lives and schooling span different countries like the United States, Canada, and Mexico, and/or countries in the Caribbean or Asia, for example.

Who are transnational students? Skerrett asks. They are not just immigrants who have left one culture for another. "Transnational students," she argues, "are those who live across two or more nations and who attend school in one or more of the nations they call home."[17]

For a long time, emigration for most people felt like a one-way ticket. From the Dutch nonconformists who became some of the first American colonists, to the convicts who were transported to Australia, to the Jews who escaped the Holocaust, as well as Dennis's own ancestors who came to the United States from England and Ireland, for example, emigration had an air of finality about it. Trips home were extremely rare or nonexistent. When you emigrated to North America, you often became an exaggerated example of your adopted culture by exchanging one sport for another or trading warm beer in the pub for cold ones out on the deck. Alternatively, you settled in enclaves consisting of people like you, such as Little Italy

SUGGESTIONS FOR CELEBRATING TRANSNATIONAL IDENTITIES

- Undertake projects on content related to students' countries of origin.

- Use students' countries of origin as a focus for the rest of the class. Who better to ask about the effects of rainforest destruction on climate change than a Brazilian student who has witnessed it firsthand?

- Continue building students' original languages while developing new ones.

- Develop "third" identities of "global citizenship that include expertise and capacities to identify, care about, critically analyze, and develop potential solutions to the social justice concerns of all people and all nations."[19]

or Chinatown, where you could continue to speak the language and engage in the customs of your home country.

Travel is cheaper and faster now. Being able to go home and back frequently is easier than it used to be. Moreover, Skerrett points out, "even when physical border-crossing is not possible, people classified as migrants employ digital and other tools to participate economically, socially, and politically in their nations of origin."[18] People can and often do feel attached to two or more countries and cultures now.

Many immigrants today connect with their families and former friends by Zoom, FaceTime, WhatsApp, and other platforms. They text each other constantly and send pictures from their phones scores of times a day. Harvard University anthropologist Gabrielle Oliveira has documented how immigrant parents remain actively involved with their children's education by using these online tools, even though economic conditions sometimes require them to be physically separated for months on end. In some large and extended families that she studied in New York City, parents regularly switch back and forth between their jobs and their iPhones, praising their children when they are doing well, and scolding them when they've gone astray.

If teachers and schools aren't aware of and attentive to the transnational aspects of students' identities, they'll see the effects of those identities as a problem or a deficit. They'll regard the sudden and unexpected disappearance of their students for weeks or months to go back to Guatemala, Brazil, or Pakistan, for instance, as simply lost schooling. So, what *can* teachers and schools do to address transnational identities in these circumstances? Skerrett suggests several strategies, summarized in the sidebar on this page.

In addition, Skerrett argues, teachers can build partnerships with the schools, communities, and teachers in their students' other countries. In some cases, perhaps, they can even visit them in vacation time.

In an age of instant communication, it's not reasonable to demand that students and their families should have a single national identity, whether that is of their country of origin or where they now live. Nor can we simply say that people should have only diffuse global identities. Some conservative criticisms of cosmopolitanism are right about this. We can't be citizens of everywhere and nowhere. Boundaries *do* matter. There can be no clear sense of identity, of being one thing rather than another, without them. Identity always entails some element of exclusion. Indeed, if everything is totally fluid and there are no senses of boundaries, it's hard to know how it is possible to have an identity at all.

Still, our identities need not be binary, and, when it comes right down to it, they rarely are. "Identity is revealed as an activity," Kwame Anthony Appiah has written, "not a thing."[20] It is no longer practical or appropriate today for countries to insist that citizens have only a single citizenship. In nationality, as in many other parts of life, we can have and should be able to embrace a both–and identity if we wish, not an either–or one.

"Imagine we can belong to *more than* one country," we might say, paraphrasing John Lennon. "It isn't hard to do!"

Mixed Heritage Identities

Trevor Noah is a South African–born acclaimed comedian and former U.S. talk-show host. In *Born a Crime*, Noah describes his upbringing as the illegally born son of a Black Xhosa mother and a white Swiss German father, in apartheid-era South Africa. Once apartheid was officially ending, Noah found himself among white students in his A-stream class, but among largely Black students out in the schoolyard. "The white kids I'd met that morning went in one direction, the black kids went in another direction, and I was left standing in the middle, totally confused," he recalls.[21] "I was everywhere with everybody, and at the same time I was all by myself." In time, Noah turned these identity strategies into political satire, which became the foundation for his talk-show career. But when someone's identity includes different elements of race or heritage, the results are not always managed so deftly.

In his autobiography *Spare*, the United Kingdom's Prince Harry documents the racism directed at his wife, Meghan Markle, Duchess of Sussex, by members of the British Royal Family.[22] Although Markle is on record as being proud of her mixed Black and white heritage, the insinuations and insults of members of the Royal Family toward the duchess betrayed their primal fears and hostility about their royal bloodline being corrupted. These peaked in 2021 when it was announced that Markle was pregnant, and members of the Royal Family expressed "concerns" over the baby's potential skin color.

Mixed heritage identity also poses a problem among many ordinary people. Old terms used to define this identity like *half-caste* or *half-breed* are particularly stigmatizing designations. They are about being less of something, and little of something purportedly better, rather than about having a richer, stronger identity overall.

Taking off from a Harry and Meghan documentary, Samantha Chery, writing in the *Washington Post* in February 2023, interviewed several women who talked about the implications of being mixed race.[23] More than 33 million Americans identify as being of two or more races, Chery notes, yet the bureaucratic paperwork of many officials, including law enforcement officers pulling people over for driving tickets, label everyone in relation to a single racial category. In some settings you're privileged, while in others you're marginalized, her interviewees remarked. "I had Black girls be very mean to me, and I had White girls be very mean to me," a graduate student commented. "Being mixed, you are in a constant battle of pleasing the Black side of you and also pleasing the White side of you and not knowing how to balance."[24] She knew just how Meghan Markle felt.

Andy's grandchildren are all mixed ethnocultural heritage. Yet, apart from the twins, perhaps, they all look quite different from each other. Andy and his wife, Pauline, have acquired and read books to them that sometimes include Asian characters, like Ling and Ting, identical twins who are very alike and are also utterly unique. They put money in red envelopes to celebrate Lunar New Year, and they also stack gifts from Santa Claus under the Christmas tree. When Jackson was about 8 years old and learning about slavery, he stroked his forearm and asked, "Has anyone like me ever been made a slave?" Then Andy and Pauline discussed how enslavement has been experienced by people of all skin colors and ethnicities, under the rule of the Greeks, the Romans, the Vikings, and the ancient Egyptians, as well as the European colonizers of the Americas, for example, right up to human trafficking in the present day. Owning people has been historically widespread, they pointed out, and is always wrong.

"People need to have more nuanced conversation about race and identity that's beyond stereotypical categories," one of Chery's respondents said.[25] In the words of another, children should "have more opportunities to learn about being multiracial through positive representation in games and books."[26] Inclusion needs to recognize multiple and mixed identities, not just purely singular ones, as sources of richness, strength, and marvelous human complexity, where heritage and ancestry still matter, and where people are also not distilled to being one single part of it and disparaged if they resist.

The late philosopher John Ralston Saul claimed that Canadian identity and its tendency in national life to search for the middle ground when it can, and to solve disputes reasonably, is Métis in nature.[27] This, he argued, is because it is a cross between and combination of Indigenous and European heritage. It is a cruel irony, of course, that this Métis mentality has not, until very recently, been applied by successive Canadian governments to how they have addressed Indigenous injustices themselves.

Cross-Class Identities

Another way in which we can feel we exist between cultures, or where we belong to both or neither of them, is when we migrate in our status from one social class to another, through education. This is what the Russian-born Harvard University sociologist and former president of the American Sociological Association Pitirim Sorokin called "social mobility."[28] Like Goffman, Sorokin had a file held on him by the FBI. But they had nothing to fear. Exiled from his homeland and threatened with death because of his anticommunist beliefs, Sorokin, the son of a traveling craftsman, was more interested in how people could advance up the social class scale compared to their parents than he was in revolutionizing the social class system. Writing in the 1920s, Sorokin defined social mobility as "relations involved in a transition of an individual . . . from one social stratum to another."[29]

The existence of social mobility is the essence of equal educational opportunity—to be able to progress irrespective of one's social and economic origins. But the cost of social mobility, even after all the hard work and struggle to achieve it, can be considerable. It can mean leaving behind, abandoning, or disparaging the culture of working-class life, for the middle-class culture of the school.

Social class is, in many ways, the invisible man or woman in contemporary discussions about identity. Race, gender, neurodiversity, nationality, and many other facets of identity rightly occupy a lot of the space

Inclusion needs to recognize multiple and mixed identities, not just purely singular ones, as sources of richness, strength, and marvelous human complexity, where heritage and ancestry still matter, and where people are also not distilled to being one single part of it and disparaged if they resist.

in discussions about equity, inclusion, and diversity. Yet social class, which, 50 years ago, was the main way that most Europeans and some Americans talked about equity—often at the cost of all these other dimensions—has, in the *Age of Identity*, now receded into the shadows. There are four reasons for this.

1. Don't Mention the White Working Class

Acknowledging the struggles of the working class might be equated with acknowledging the *white* working class. That would risk associating whiteness with disadvantage instead of with its historic racial privilege. The coronavirus crisis, though, made it clear that the working class is actually very diverse. Essential workers include migrant farm laborers, immigrant home care workers, hospital cleaners, Uber drivers, and waitstaff. Whatever their race or ethnicity, they are all members of the working class who are engaged with manual or other routine labor (like working in a call center). They have the low pay and contractual insecurities to prove it. Working-class identity intersects with many other aspects of diversity—something we discuss in more detail in the next chapter. Social class is not an exception to or enemy of diversity. It is part of diversity. It needs to come back into the overall reckoning about inequality and exclusion.

2. We're All Middle Class Now

Joan Williams, author of *White Working Class*, says that the United States has become "clueless" about social class.[30] It is not alone. Canada has its own (working-class) cluelessness, expressed in the widespread belief that most Canadians are *middle class*. "Most Canadians think of themselves as middle class," says Julie Cazzin in a 2017 edition of *Maclean's* magazine.[31] Around 70% of Canadians self-identify as middle class, according to the magazine's poll. In another *Maclean's* article, Shannon Proudfoot warns that "the way we elide, erase and ignore socioeconomic class in Canada" makes it "like an invisible fact that shapes everything, but is acknowledged nowhere."[32] "Conflating class in Canada" and "making everybody middle class who isn't rich" is "maybe more dangerous than having some awareness of class," says Canadian sociology professor Wolfgang Lehmann.[33] Our schools must grant as much dignity to the labor and values of working-class life as they do to other aspects of identity. Furthermore, just as confronting the oppression of racial and ethnic minorities requires us to talk about white privilege, addressing the marginalization of working-class identities requires us to talk about wealth privilege.

3. Working Class Equals Poor

Poverty continues to have massive consequences for student achievement and well-being. Several of our districts instituted a wide array of antipoverty strategies. But, unless you're Dolly Parton, it is almost impossible to turn poverty on its head and celebrate it in the way we do with Black Power, Gay Pride, and other kinds of diversity. And being working class is about more than having low income. Skilled manual labor had dignity and worth up to the 1970s, including financially. Working-class labor and communities were a source of collective pride. Historically, trade unions have brought about more equal pay for women, health and safety protections for workers, and democracy and solidarity movements in eastern Europe. Where in our curriculum is the history of labor, labor rights, and trade unions, alongside business entrepreneurship and financial literacy? Inclusion should encompass *social class* inclusion. The labor, culture, skills, and pride of working-class identity must be acknowledged with dignity.

4. Class Is a Position, Not an Identity

Getting to grips with working-class identity raises the question of what it means to move up and out of the working class, through education, into middle-class work and life. In his memoir, *Moving*, of growing up in a working-class community, Andy describes how he failed to get a good enough grade in his history exam to get him into university at the first attempt, because of a curriculum that had been made up of "kings and queens, popes, and generals . . . in what was a history of the ruling classes (that) meant very little" to him.[34] With his widowed mother receiving government financial assistance, Andy took on three part-time jobs on two nights a week and for a day and a half on the weekend. He also wanted to stay connected to his working-class friends in his community, so he would play sports with them in the local park in the evenings. Only after meeting these other obligations and commitments did he start his homework, after everyone else had gone to bed.

Wolfgang Lehmann interviewed Canadian students from working-class backgrounds who managed to be academically successful. These students, in the words of his *Maclean's* magazine interviewer, "no longer fit in where they used to, but there were still moments when they would feel like cultural outsiders in their new world, too."[35] Upwardly mobile students from the working class can too easily be made to feel like their culture and identity of origin is profane, coarse, trashy, or completely invisible and should be left behind.

Cross-Class Identity Summary

Three of our 10 districts were traditional working-class communities based in industries like steelwork, auto manufacturing, and chocolate production. They had made many important moves to enhance student engagement and well-being in technological innovation, organizing sponsored walks to support mental health and LGBTQ+ rights, studying the lives and culture of historic African Canadians, being inclusive and welcoming to refugee families, developing resiliency, and so on. Yet none of these districts displayed any attention to the identities of the working class, or identities that were embedded in work.

Fast-forward a few years, however, and craft skills and vocational education are being reinvented. Cardboard, metalwork, woodwork, and plastics have progressed into design thinking, robotics, 3D printers, and makerspace classrooms. As nations bring manufacturing closer to home in response to the disruption of supply chains caused by the pandemic and other factors, the craft skills of working-class labor are making a comeback. Makerspace education, long associated with boys, is rightly being celebrated for its suitability for girls. Now is also the time for bringing these traditional working-class competencies for making things into middle-class life. Why isn't there a social class version of the diversity principle that what is essential for some kids is good for all of them?

An hour's drive out of Canada's capital city of Ottawa, a high school participating in the Playful Schools Network that Andy codirects has connected its chosen innovations to the needs of its working-class students. In a town with 10% unemployment and 25% low-income families, this school is striving to make sure that students see their value to the community, even though they are often hungry and stressed. It is teaching students about nutrition, cooking, and planning for meals in ways that involve budgeting, planting, grocery shopping, and distributing food to the community.

In a predominantly white working-class town battling incidents of racism, students are also learning to engage with and enjoy different and unfamiliar cuisines. They are meeting with diverse owners of local restaurants. They are comparing food prices among food suppliers. They are creating their own high-quality digital recipes with linked QR codes to musical soundtracks so that, as they say, when you're cooking, "you don't just feed your body, you need to feed your soul."

A related innovation in this school is its "grow towers." These are new technologies for cultivating vegetables indoors. They need light, irrigation, and other features to be successful. Grow towers are especially valuable during long, hard winters in northern climates. The school originally purchased a grow tower from project funds and proudly displayed it to the students. One Grade 7 boy who had recently been excluded for several weeks for fighting asked how much this tower had cost. When he learned that the school had paid $1,200, he proclaimed that he and his father could make it for a fraction of the cost. They then did just that, using craft skills that were fundamental parts of their working-class identities.

Now, students are building their own grow towers in the school's atrium to provide fruits and vegetables for the community. The youth who had previously been marginalized for disruptive behavior was not merely included now. He was a leader of other students and their teachers.

This is one striking example of how schools can value and include the skills and motivations of working-class identity. The dignity of manual labor, and of craft skills, in the community is now visible to everyone in the entrance to the school. All that is missing is a clear connection of these skills to historic aspects of working-class identity, similar to how skills such as learning on the land are explicitly related to Indigenous identities, for example.

Work is a significant part of many people's identities. When we start dating or just strike up conversations with strangers, isn't the question "What do you do?" one of the very first that we ask? Work is central to who we are. Why exclude it from the curriculum or from discussions about identity? Our schools must accord as much dignity to the values of working-class lives and labor as they do to other aspects of identity. Neither they nor the rest of us should make young people with working-class identities feel that they must leave behind or give up who they are in order to be socially mobile, and to enter into the ranks of middle-class life. Going back and forth between social class identities needn't condemn anyone to crossing over a one-way divide.

Transforming Identities

In a rational, equitable, and inclusive world, we must start to value identities that are combinations and transformations of other identities not as losses or compromises, but as gains and valuable new creations in their own right. This must be done whether these are combinations and transformations according to nationality, race, class, gender, age, or any other criterion. We must start to see multiple and mixed identities

> Our schools must accord as much dignity to the values of working-class lives and labor as they do to other aspects of identity.

> Going back and forth between social class identities needn't condemn anyone to crossing over a one-way divide.

not as transitional between existing forms, but as new, transformational forms altogether. Yet this often seems so hard to do. Why?

Societies and their powerful elites are often averse to mixing up human categories that had hitherto been kept apart. There are two reasons for this: *purity* and *power*. Mary Douglas, one of the most esteemed anthropologists of all time, wrote a classic book on *Purity and Danger: An Analysis of Concepts of Pollution and Taboo*.[36] It has been listed by *The Times Literary Supplement* as one of the 100 most influential nonfiction books published since the Second World War. It has been cited over 30,000 times.

Douglas was interested in how societies of all kinds engaged in and established *boundary maintenance* between what was clean or pure and unclean or dirty. These oppositions, Douglas said, gave societies a sense of moral purpose and organization. Douglas believed there is a collective human need to establish firm boundaries—especially those that relate to openings of our bodies that are involved in what we eat, drink, and eat; how we excrete; and whether and how we copulate.

The British sociologist and curriculum theorist Basil Bernstein was a friend and intellectual adversary of Douglas. Like Douglas, Bernstein was interested in how things went together or were kept apart, and in how people felt when their treasured categories were polluted. But he was also interested in power as well as purity. He wanted to know what happened when boundaries weakened and then seemed to pose threats to existing orders of power and control. A moment's reflection on some contemporary examples reveals the importance of this interest.

Opposition to mixed (interracial) marriages is stoked by fears that the purity of blood and bloodlines will be corrupted. Elites often resent those who are upwardly mobile because they get above themselves and move up where they don't belong. Populists present "asylum-seeking" immigrants as invaders who are replacing the pure heritage of the existing nation. Transgender individuals with fluid identities threaten traditional masculine power on the one hand, and challenge what some feminists believe are their hard-won rights and protections as women on the other. Some people regard retirement, the end of work, and old age as just a waiting room for the end of life, rather than having importance, meaning, and dignity in its own right.

Adolescents are neither children nor adults and are therefore denied a voice of their own. Also, in Northern Ireland and elsewhere, it was not all that long ago that mixed-faith marriages between Catholics and

Protestants could lead to banishment and worse by one's family and community. Impurity is so often regarded by the powerful as a danger and a threat.

Bernstein's interest was in how purity and power play out in the school curriculum. The way the curriculum is organized, he said, "reflects both the distribution of power and the principles of social control" in society.[37] When clearly defined school subjects like English, science, and history are separated by strong boundaries, he argued, this supports and perpetuates existing structures of power and control. Strong boundaries preserve disciplines of traditional, abstract knowledge that is unrelated to students' everyday lives and that serves the interests of elites who benefit from it. Like Andy's high school history course, a curriculum that has little relevance to working-class life favors the privileged.

Weak boundaries, by contrast, blur the differences between subjects. By polluting existing knowledge distinctions, they weaken the grip of powerful groups on learning, achievement, and pathways to success. Weak boundaries are tolerated and even welcomed in kindergarten, or in alternative or low-track programs to motivate lower achievers. However, when students get closer to honors classes, the final years of high school, and college entrance, the abstract, subject-based curriculum becomes more strictly bounded and exclusionary. The gateways to success are guarded more closely.

Subjects and subject contents are linked to identity, opportunity, and success. Blurring and mixture of categories challenges this. "Any attempt to weaken or change" subject boundaries, Bernstein argued, "may be felt as a threat to one's identity *and may be experienced as pollution.*"[38] These movements lead to "a disturbance of existing authority structures" and the grip they have on knowledge and gateways to success. All this explains why interdisciplinary or project-based learning for all students, or alternative forms of assessment, can provoke incredible degrees of resistance.

This is not just an academic argument. In the late 19th century in the United States and the early 20th century in the United Kingdom, the growing social mobility of the working class prompted reactions by governments and some university elites to try and redefine the secondary school curriculum in classical and abstract terms.[39] Subjects like Latin and Greek were presented as being essential to university access. Political pleas to go back to basics or reinstate traditional canons are the modern reinvention of these reactions.

One of the explanations for a shift toward weaker curriculum boundaries is when there is greater egalitarianism and inclusion in the wider society, Bernstein argued. This might illuminate why movements toward project-based learning, sustainable development goals, and global competencies in education today are happening alongside efforts to install gender-neutral bathrooms, advance special education inclusion, decolonize the curriculum, broaden the criteria for college admissions, and increase culturally responsive teaching. It might also explain countermovements to remove nontraditional families from students' literacy materials, foment moral panics about transgender bathrooms, block honors courses on subjects like African American history, put an end to positive discrimination practices in college admissions, and reinstate historical study of imperial figures.

The answer to bad boundaries is not no boundaries, though. Weakened boundaries can be highly generative for new ways of understanding and relating to one another. But they still involve boundaries.

A world of no boundaries, weak or strong, is a world in which we have no confidence or clarity about who we are or where we are going. This does not transform existing identities. It obliterates them. Erickson understood that identity formation is about developing and then transforming bounded senses of who we are. Better boundaries, based on clear and agreed-upon principles of both inclusion *and* equity, are what we should be creating: a topic we return to in the final chapter.

> A world of no boundaries is a world in which we have no confidence or clarity about who we are or where we are going. This does not transform existing identities. It obliterates them.

BEYOND DIVIDED SELVES

We've learned some important things in this chapter and this book about our selves and our identities. Selves don't exist within us, as if they are timeless spiritual souls. They are human constructions, products of how societies evolve and change.

Our selves are social. They are the result of the relationships we have with people we value—like our parents, our teachers, our peers, and, today, the *influencers* on social media. But societies and communities can be oppressive toward these selves, as well as nurturing of them. Tragically, some people are driven to display false and divided selves so they can evade censure and stigmatization.

Having multiple identities isn't always problematic or pathological. Modern societies involve us in countless relationships and interactions.

We put on different performances in varied settings—frontstage and backstage, online and offline, formal and intimate. Ideally, we can find ways to enjoy all these roles and view them as opportunities for engaging with other people in the fullness of their personalities, just as they come to appreciate the many different sides that we exhibit in our everyday lives.

People no longer need to be just one thing, or nothing at all. Butterflies and moths are not failed caterpillars. They are transformational beings, in their own right. Likewise, people can be transnational, transgender, mixed heritage, or whatever else they really want to be. They can combine and even fuse their different identities in ways that make sense to them. But to do this calls for not just willpower or effort. It requires collective clarity about principles and boundaries that can guide us all.

Multiple identities can be our allies. They need not be our adversaries. We all already have multiple identities. This should give us fellowship with others. The complications of multiple identities needn't make us feel despondent or defeated. They can increase our creativity, enable us to learn from diversity, and expand our humanity. In the final chapter, we set out some principles and strategies for how we can learn to live together with and across very different and diverse identities, rather than setting ourselves against one another or driving each other apart. For now, we will move our analysis of multiple identities one step further into the realm of what is known as *intersecting* identities.

Notes

1. Beah, I. (2008). *A long way gone: Memoirs of a boy soldier.* Farrar, Straus, & Giroux.
2. Lewis, S. (2013, January 13). *Keynote address to Ontario College of Teachers.* https://www.oct.ca/resources/videos/stephen-lewis
3. Appiah, K. A. (2005). *The ethics of identity.* Princeton University Press; Jenkins, R. (2014). *Social identity.* Routledge.
4. Mackenzie, C., & Stoljar, N. (Eds.). (2000). *Relational autonomy: Feminist perspectives on autonomy, agency, and the social self.* Oxford University Press.
5. American Psychiatric Association. (2022). *What are dissociative disorders?* https://www.psychiatry.org/patients-families/dissociative-disorders/what-are-dissociative-disorders
6. Goffman's FBI record was first uncovered by Shalin, D. N. (2016). Erving Goffman, fateful action, and the Las Vegas gambling scene. *UNLV Gaming Research and Review Journal, 20*(1), 1–38.

7. Goffman, E. (1959). *The presentation of self in everyday life.* Anchor.
8. Ibid., p. 12.
9. Shakespeare, W. (1940). *Five great tragedies.* Pocket Books, p. 513. (Original work published 1623)
10. Goffman, *Presentation of self in everyday life,* p. 48.
11. Ibid., p. 128.
12. Ibid.
13. Valenzuela, A. (2008). Uncovering internalized oppression. In M. Pollock (Ed.), *Everyday antiracism* (pp. 50–54). New Press, quote from p. 52.
14. Ibid., quote from p. 50.
15. Ibid., quote from p. 52.
16. Ibid., quote from p. 54.
17. Skerrett, A. (2020). Transnational students and educational change. *Journal of Educational Change, 21,* 499–509, quote from p. 499.
18. Ibid., quote from p. 500.
19. Ibid., quote from p. 504.
20. Appiah, K. A. (2018). *The lies that bind: Rethinking identity.* Liveright, p. 67.
21. Noah, T. (2018). *Born a crime: Stories from a South African childhood.* Spiegel & Grau, p. 57.
22. Prince Harry. (2023). *Spare.* Random House.
23. Chery, S. (2023, February 18). Biracial women say Meghan is proof that racism and privilege coexist. *The Washington Post.* https://www.washingtonpost.com/lifestyle/2023/02/18/biracial-racism-meghan-markle-identity/
24. Ibid.
25. Ibid.
26. Ibid.
27. Saul, J. R. (2009). *A fair country: Telling truths about Canada.* Penguin Canada.
28. Sorokin, P. (1959). *Social and cultural mobility.* Free Press, p. 133. (Original work published 1927)
29. Ibid.
30. Williams, J. C. (2017). *White working class: Overcoming class cluelessness in America.* Harvard Business Press, p. 2.
31. Cazzin, J. (2017, June 16). Why everyone feels like they're in the middle class. *Maclean's.* https://macleans.ca/economy/why-everyone-feels-like-theyre-in-the-middle-class/
32. Proudfoot, S. (2019, July 16). What does it mean to be working class in Canada? *Maclean's.* https://macleans.ca/society/what-does-it-mean-to-be-working-class-in-canada/
33. Lehmann is quoted in Proudfoot, What does it mean to be working class in Canada?
34. Hargreaves, A. (2020). *Moving: A memoir of education and social mobility.* Solution Tree, p. 99.
35. Lehmann is quoted in Proudfoot, What does it mean to be working class in Canada?
36. Douglas, M. (1966). *Purity and danger: An analysis of concepts of pollution and taboo.* Routledge.
37. Bernstein, B. (1975). *Class, codes, and control: Vol. 3. Towards a theory of educational transmissions.* Routledge, p. 85.
38. Ibid., p. 96.
39. Goodson, I. (1995). *The making of curriculum: Collected essays.* RoutledgeFalmer.

CHAPTER 6

Intersecting Identities

"I defined myself in opposition to my father. . . . When he said he was Pakistani, I declared I was British; he was Muslim, I was confused; he believed in family, I championed the individual; he worshipped money, I claimed it meant nothing."

—From *Greetings From Bury Park* by Sarfraz Manzoor (2008)

Good teachers know that they can't just ask the students to conform to the school, but that they also should adapt the school to the students.

Inspecting Intersections

In the popular 2019 movie *Blinded by the Light*, the protagonist, Javed, a teenage son of a strict and traditional Pakistani-Muslim family that has immigrated to England, goes through many identity conflicts and transformations.[1] The film is based on a memoir by Sarfraz Manzoor, who describes himself as "an unemployed British Pakistani with shoulder-length dreadlocks, a silver nose ring and a strange fascination with Bruce Springsteen."[2]

In the movie, Javed is out of place in both his school and his family. Then, through his relationship with another South Asian student in the school, a Sikh boy, he becomes acquainted with the white working-class American rock music star Bruce Springsteen. As well as understanding that rock music might feed his appetite for attracting girls, this hitherto traditional Muslim boy who, along with his family, experiences racist abuse from white youths in the community, finds in Springsteen's lyrics of white working-class life an affinity that is grounded in their common struggle against isolation, inequality, and oppression.

Part of Javed's complex identity is his adolescence. His culturally conservative parents don't understand his fascination with this "Jewish man" Springsteen—a moment of delightful irony in the movie script. They just want him to study hard and be successful in his career. In addition, they want him to marry a Pakistani girl that they have planned to select for him.

Springsteen's life in and lyrics about white working-class America throw a light on Javed's suffering—a light that nearly blinds him. The music, the pleasure it brings, and the escape it offers from parochial mediocrity and prejudice-ridden misery is so intense that when Javed finally heads off to buy tickets to see Springsteen perform in person, he neglects his sister's traditional wedding. As he makes his way to the train station, he is also oblivious to acts of racist violence against his family's wedding party.

Eventually, just in time, Javed sees the light, and instead of continuing to act as a bystander with better things to do, he steps into the fray as a son and a brother. In the movie's concluding epiphany, when Javed receives a writing award at his school, his father, mother, and sister show up just in time, at the back of the hall, to hear Javed read his winning entry. But instead of reading his essay, Javed articulates how its substance connects him to his family's struggles. "I like your stories," Javed's father says to him at the end. "But," he adds, "don't forget our stories too!"

Blinded by the Light portrays the essential hope that exists on the other side of multiple identities. It is not a political statement about irreconcilable identities, Muslim and Sikh, Brown and white, or old and young in a combative language of indignation about the privileges held by some or the special treatments afforded to others. Writing in *The Guardian*, Manzoor reflected on how "I could not have predicted that Israeli women in Jerusalem, white teenage American boys in Omaha, Nebraska and older white women in Australia would all contact me . . . and thank me for telling their story."[3]

Blinded by the Light represents the struggle toward establishing a shared humanity that leaves multiple identities intact, but also brings them together in rich new combinations. It is a compelling portrayal of the complexity of the idea that we all "contain multitudes," in the words of poet Walt Whitman.[4]

The basic idea about multiple selves and identities has been moved to another level of conceptual sophistication and strategic intensity by a new academic term that has now also entered popular and political discourse: *intersectionality*. We even heard Ontario Premier Kathleen Wynne use it.

Intersectionality was introduced by African American legal scholar and feminist theorist Kimberlé Crenshaw in 1989.[5] Crenshaw defines intersectionality as "a lens through which you can see where power comes and collides, where it interlocks and intersects. It's not simply that there's a race problem here, a gender problem here, and a class or LGBTQ+ problem there. Many times, that framework erases what happens to people who are subject to all these things."[6] Intersectionality lends the core idea of multiple identities a sharply critical edge by exploring the ways in which power affects all human relationships.

The rest of this chapter explains the nature and importance of Crenshaw's concept. It then moves beyond her original work, and draws on our own research evidence, to encompass three forms of intersectionality: *critical* (in line with her original argument), *constructive*, and *conflicting*.

Critical Intersectionality

Crenshaw is a professor at the UCLA School of Law and Columbia Law School. In the 1980s, she undertook a case study of a battered women's shelter in Los Angeles. She was concerned that even from a feminist perspective, women who were victims of domestic violence were represented as encountering the same kind of problem that focused exclusively on their gender. The comparative neglect of race and other targets of oppressors, she argued, led to a systemic neglect of the specific situation and oppression of Black women.

In her widely cited 1989 paper for the *University of Chicago Legal Forum* on "Demarginalizing the Intersection of Race and Sex: A Black Feminist Critique of Antidiscrimination Doctrine, Feminist Theory and Antiracist Politics," Crenshaw pointed out that a white middle-class woman who had been the victim of domestic violence was positioned differently in terms of how she could access resources and how people responded to her, compared to an impoverished Black woman, who might not have English as her first language and might also be an undocumented immigrant.[7] Even some strategies intended to help the woman, Crenshaw argued, unintentionally exacerbated her social marginalization. "Black women are sometimes excluded from feminist theory and antiracist policy discourse," Crenshaw explained, "because both are predicated on a discrete set of experiences that often does not accurately reflect the intersection of race and gender."[8]

These kinds of intersections are not random, Crenshaw insisted. Why are some students punished more often and more severely than others? Why do some young people recover from drug addiction more readily than others? Why do some students with special needs get all the assistance they need, whereas others receive minimal support or less? Powerlessness is a toxic human compound in the periodic table of life. That's what Crenshaw helps us to see.

> Powerlessness is a toxic human compound in the periodic table of life.

In 1990, University of Maryland professor Patricia Hill Collins argued that intersectionality is embedded in and expresses a dynamic "matrix of domination."[9] For Collins, the combined forces of race, gender, class, sexuality, and nationality overlap and provide "particular forms of intersecting oppressions" that "cannot be reduced to one fundamental type."[10] If we really want to understand the essence of what it means to be oppressed, Collins says, we have to refrain from simplistic explanations and see how various forms of marginalization conspire to push people to the edges of their societies.

The cruel reality that critical intersectionality exposes requires that we confront the persistent and pervasive educational inequalities experienced by multiply marginalized groups, such as Indigenous students who live in poverty or gay Black boys who are bullied, for example. Understanding the powerful impact of intersectionality entails a kind of "matrix thinking" about societies and school systems.[11] This requires educators to replace strings of isolated interventions with responses to young people as whole people who experience multiple challenges and forms of oppression at the same time.

We observed what we call *critical intersectionality* in how schools in the 10 districts we studied were addressing the tragic history of Canadian residential schools and their impact on students and their families. Residential schools have bequeathed a shameful legacy to Indigenous communities. Intergenerational trauma originating in neglect, violence, and abuse by teachers, priests, nuns, and other caregivers has been passed on to children and grandchildren of the original victims. "We're now in that generation where their parents were in residential school systems," one principal said. "It's a mess. It really is." This remark is not a casual imputation of a deficit. It's an indictment of systemic oppression.

Students in Indigenous communities we studied struggled not just because of their race, as if that was not enough, but also because of the intersection of appalling levels of poverty and profound degrees of psychological trauma. The lesson of critical intersectionality is not to focus on a singular aspect of students' marginalized identities, and not to oversimplify problems as being exclusively or predominantly ones of race, or poverty, or second-language learning, or post-traumatic stress among the children of recently immigrated refugees, for example. Educational leaders do not operate in blind controlled research studies. They do not deal with one variable at a time. They need to look at the whole child who experiences problems in complex bundles of critical intersectionality, just as Crenshaw and Collins argued.

For example, refugees who come into Canada don't just need help with learning English or French, or even compensation for missed years of schooling. They typically also are poor, belong to visible minority groups, and have post-traumatic stress disorders or other special needs. Responding to refugees and other newcomers, therefore, is about joining up the supports across and among whole communities of educators for groups of children and adolescents who have multiple challenges, including adapting to their identities as new Canadians.

Critical intersectionality calls upon us to think hard about how we classify and label students. It asks us to consider whether how we do this restricts us to narrow technical interventions that don't get at the root causes of students' difficulties. It requires us to look closely at which groups of students are subject to higher rates of referral and suspension and to ask ourselves why. It demands that we resist the temptations to just make swift data-driven interventions, and that we turn to in-depth discussions of which students we're losing, and why, instead.

For educators who think the key to student engagement is filling the curriculum with fun and joy, critical intersectionality doesn't offer many options. Although it does invite us to look at the strengths and assets that students and their identities bring to school with them, and not just their problems and difficulties, it is frankly no fun at all to teach about the horrors of the residential school system, the murders that led to the Black Lives Matter movement, or the maltreatment of refugees. There's no joy in discussing the high suicide rates of LGBTQ+ students or the rising "deaths of despair" among the white working class. Critical intersectionality is daunting but necessary. It offers fulfillment even though there is not much pleasure in it. It also requires us to look at these kinds of social problems and the sources of marginalization and oppression behind them not as isolated issues needing single interventions, but as reflections of matrices of domination that implicate us all.

Constructive Intersectionality

The flip side of *critical intersectionality* is *constructive intersectionality*. To get a good grip on its nature, let's turn to popular culture and the music industry.

Canada's iconic rap artist and all-round music star, Drake, is a four-time Grammy Award winner and U.S. Billboard chart-topper. He's known to all demographics: young and old, Black and white. Drake is a beloved Canadian who is proud of his roots and loyal to them.

What is Drake's identity? Obviously, like most rap stars, he's Black. But Drake insists this isn't the only thing about him. As well as being Black, Drake is Jewish. He's a basketball fan. And he's a passionate advocate for *the 416*—the phone area code of his lifelong hometown, Toronto.[12]

This last aspect of Drake's identity might seem trivial to readers who are not Canadian, but by signaling its importance to all his fans, Drake is also making a radical statement. In the generation before Drake, Canadian entertainers, like musicians Joni Mitchell and Neil Young or comedians Martin Short and Mike Myers (of *Austin Powers* fame), felt they had to go to Hollywood to make the big time. But Drake, like a whole generation of music stars following him, is asserting his national and cultural identity as a Canadian artist against the dominance of Americans in the entertainment industry.

Talking up *the 416* is not a quirky curiosity. It's a countercultural assertion of a hitherto marginalized identity against American cultural domination. Drake is saying that he can be a successful entertainer

[Critical intersectionality] requires us to look at the sources of marginalization and oppression not as isolated issues needing single interventions, but as reflections of matrices of domination that implicate us all.

without having to give up being Canadian. He understands this resistant narrative because he came from a humble background where, as his song lyrics testify, he "started from the bottom. Now my whole team ****ing here."[13]

What would Drake look like if he were not a person, but a school instead? The school and the people in it would refuse to be defined by a single identity, especially a stigmatized one associated with deficits. People with learning disabilities would practice self-advocacy. Newcomers would bring additional, enriching elements to the school that benefit everyone. Festivals and faiths would be celebrated, including ones that are less fashionable and perhaps not even always politically correct.

We've seen examples of constructive intersectionality throughout this book. When a teacher understood that a student's identity as both a linguistic minority and an immigrant could be leveraged to teach a word of Arabic to his classmates every day, she was tapping into constructive intersectionality. When the francophone district's coordinator for *safe and inclusive schools* provided professional learning and development for teachers so they could welcome students from all races and countries to her district—despite the inevitable transformation of traditional Franco-Ontarian culture that would result—she was putting constructive intersectionality to work. Teachers in northwestern Ontario were also using constructive intersectionality when they adjusted their pedagogies to their Indigenous students' learning disabilities by constructing climbing walls in the classroom for them to expend surplus energy on.

Good teachers know that they can't just ask the students to conform to the school, but that they also should adapt the school to the students. Constructive intersectionality takes this principle further by pointing to the multiple and converging assets that make up students' identities. When educators work on interdisciplinary teams and bring all their knowledge of the students into one conversation, constructive intersectionality becomes a way for everyone to identify the multiple and overlapping strengths that each student brings to their learning and their school.

Conflicting Intersectionality

Asserting different identities isn't always straightforward or unambiguously positive. When newcomers first arrive, they may have different views from majority Canadians, or from any liberal democracy, about religion, gender equity, racism, or LGBTQ+ identity, for example. This raises questions not just about accepting people's identities as they are, but also about engaging with those identities in the human rights context of the host society and the Universal Declaration of Human Rights as well. Some ways of expressing identities can seem positive in terms of cultural pluralism, but they can also pose problems for the exclusion of others. How can educators deal with these? Here we enter a complicated and controversial terrain of conflicted intersectionality that practically everyone recognizes but that too many leaders are either unhelpfully evasive or excessively judgmental about.

The challenge and opportunity of *learning to live together* is greater inclusion. But when we come up against conflicting forms of intersectionality that juxtapose positive and problematic aspects of people's identities, we often descend into the accusatory indignation of identity politics or into lily-livered dispositions of evasive leadership. There are ways to proceed beyond this point. But we will need open minds, generous hearts, and strong wills to do so.

Alex Scott is a Black British TV sports commentator and former soccer star. Featured in a 2021 episode of *Who Do You Think You Are?* she was horrified and broke down in tears when she was presented with records showing that one of her ancestors, although Black himself, had been an owner of 26 slaves. "He was an owner of people?" she asked, in shock and exasperation. "That goes against everything I stand for—who I am.[14]"

Scott had not known that Black people who were freed slaves, or the offspring of freed slaves, could own slaves too. Discovering this part of her past raised fundamental questions about her identity. She was forced to confront unpleasant aspects of herself and who she was descended from. Her self-declared life story had been that she had overcome adversity and inequality on her path to success. Now she had to come to terms with also being a descendant of people who had not only been oppressed but who, as owners of people, were oppressors themselves.

Conflicting intersectionality is everywhere. People who are privileged in some respects may be marginalized in others. Some people come from families or cultures that have been both oppressors and oppressed. Like British prime minister Rishi Sunak or the Egyptian former owner of the Harrods department store, the late Mohamed Al-Fayed, you may have immense wealth privilege, but still lack white privilege. Conversely, like millions of members of the poor white working class in the

United States or United Kingdom, or like the British convicts who were transported to Australia, you may have zero wealth privilege, but still retain white privilege in encounters with Indigenous groups or other racial minorities. You may be marginalized and have been exiled from your home country because of your faith, but also bring misogynistic and homophobic attitudes to your host country.

Members of poor white working-class communities can be xenophobic and racist (Andy writes as someone who comes from one of the most pro-Brexit towns in the United Kingdom); hence, some people hesitate to acknowledge this group's legitimate economic grievances. But white working-class xenophobia is not the only example of conflicting intersectionality. There has been a tendency to suppress the relatively high recorded rates of intimate partner violence in gay and lesbian relationships because this may reinforce negative stereotypes.[15] Several faith-based communities marginalize gender-based minorities. Trans activists and some feminists, like the Harry Potter series author, J. K. Rowling, cannot agree on what is, truly, a woman, and on whether the term *birthing people* is emancipatory or oppressive. People who identify as bisexual often find themselves between two worlds, where they are fully accepted by neither gay nor straight communities. These are examples of what we call "conflicting human rights." They are based upon juxtaposed and sometimes jarring identities that should not be denied or overlooked.

> People who are privileged in some respects may be marginalized in others. Some people come from families or cultures that have been both oppressors and oppressed.

Then there is the paradox of the United States' famed *buffalo soldiers*. Named by the Indigenous peoples of the Great Plains, these six cavalry regiments of African Americans were established by Congress in 1866 and continued in operation until the Korean War.[16] Proud of their identity and their reputation for bravery, these soldiers were celebrated for their rebellious spirit in the lyrics of Bob Marley and the Wailers for the fact that they were "stolen from Africa, brought to America" to "fight on arrival," yet ended up "fighting for survival."[17] However, alongside their undoubted strengths were duties of assisting and protecting settlers in colonization and settlement of lands taken from Native Americans.

Conversely, a 2018 article in the *Smithsonian* magazine describes how the Cherokee Native Americans, who were pushed westward by President Andrew Jackson on the infamous Trail of Tears, were accompanied by their African American slaves, or had their slaves shipped in cramped boats ahead of time to Oklahoma.[18]

One of the biggest educational controversies in Birmingham, England, just before COVID-19, was a conflict between an openly lesbian headteacher (equivalent to a U.S. school principal) and a Muslim parents' group who found inclusion of LGBTQ+ sexuality and lifestyles in curriculum materials offensive to their religious beliefs and family values.[19] Asian American parents in the United States are sometimes at loggerheads with Black and Hispanic communities over the role of testing, Advanced Placement classes in high schools, and affirmative action in higher education. Dennis has studied schools in Texas that commemorated Mexican Independence Day every September, leaving the immigrant students from Honduras, Nicaragua, El Salvador, and Guatemala wondering why none of their national holidays were celebrated in the same way.

Racism is always wrong, no matter how it shows its colors. In response to discrimination by higher caste Brahmins of lower caste Dalits among Indian groups, California has proposed legislation to put an end to caste-based racism.[20] A 2023 U.K. survey report on racism and ethnic inequality found that Gypsy/Traveler/Roma and Jewish people are the groups most likely to report being racially abused, followed by Black Caribbean and Irish people.[21] In U.K. politics, Home Secretary Suella Braverman, of Hindu Tamil Mauritian and Kenyan Indian ancestry, has been criticized for inflaming Islamophobic sentiment by falsely claiming that the perpetrators of sexual grooming gangs of young girls are "almost all British-Pakistani."[22]

These are the complications of conflicting intersectionality. How do we handle them? Is a deeply problematic part of some group or individual's identity that is otherwise meritorious something we should overlook, or should it be regarded as a basis for vetoing or canceling all the individual or group's other accomplishments? Or can we hold strengths and weaknesses side by side—not in balance, necessarily, but in some sort of critical relationship? When do we connect, when do we cancel, and when do we critique?

Dilemmas and controversies concerning different aspects of conflicting intersectionality must be openly and courageously addressed by all educators now. To do so, we turn next to three examples from Ontario's schools.

Racism is always wrong, no matter how it shows its colors.

Can we hold strengths and weaknesses side by side—not in balance, necessarily, but in some sort of critical relationship?

FROM THE FIELD: TRADITIONAL ANABAPTIST BELIEFS VERSUS MODERN SECULAR VALUES

Jeremy Cassidy is a graduate of the master's degree program in education at the University of Ottawa. He was raised in a family with devout beliefs in the Pentecostal branch of Protestantism. Growing up in a close-knit faith community and attending private Christian schools, Cassidy had accepted "a life centered in trust in Jesus Christ" as "the bread and butter" of his "spiritual development."[23] When he attended university, however, he found himself "in an entirely different world." It wasn't that his faith was overtly challenged by anyone; it was more that he experienced "a startling lack of curiosity" among his classmates about his faith or what it takes to lead a meaningful life.[24]

The schism that Cassidy encountered at university led him to question the kind of education that Ontario's students were receiving on religious matters in the public schools. The core findings of his master's thesis are that Ontario's secondary school curriculum treats religion as "worthy but optional" and of "effective irrelevance to recent Canadian national history."[25] Curriculum theorists would say that religion is a part of Ontario's "null curriculum," which refers to topics that are excluded from formal academic study. Considering his own upbringing and that of the millions of not only Protestants, but people of faith around the world, Cassidy worries that there is "something amiss, broadly speaking, about a curriculum discussing contemporary Canadian history without reference to religion."[26]

McGill University professor Charles Taylor sees a broader cultural pattern in the absence of religious topics from the curriculum in schools. Taylor says that we are now living in "a secular age," which proclaims neutrality when it comes to people's personal beliefs, but then replaces religious commitment with social norms that promote the smooth functioning of capitalism.[27] We can see this, for example, in the push for "global competencies" that prepare the workforce of the future.

What does this cultural transformation toward a secular society mean in relation to small, but nonetheless important, faith communities that appear in any of the major Abrahamic religions of Judaism, Christianity, or Islam? One of our districts served a settlement of Old Order Mennonites, who began immigration into Ontario in the late 18th century. Mennonites belong to a group of traditional Christian religious groups known as Anabaptists that also include Hutterites and Amish groups in the United States. Old Order Mennonites—unlike their modernized counterparts who are, in appearance and language, largely indistinguishable from the rest of society—speak a dialect called Plattdeutsch, a reference to their flatland area of origin in the borderlands that straddle Germany and Holland. Most of the newcomers were involved in small-scale agriculture. The pursuit of freedom of their particular kind of Protestantism, and their exemption from military service, made Canada an attractive destination for this resolutely independent and pacifist culture.[28] Today, this group makes up approximately 7% of the district's population.

In traditional Mennonite culture, young people left the school system when they turned 14 years old, to help their communities with farming and household chores. Even today, formal education is not a priority. Consequently, many children have minimal English or literacy skills upon entering kindergarten. Some parents delay their children's entry to school until first grade. Many parents are illiterate and cannot read to their children at home.[29] Overall, in regard to formal education, this group is one of the most marginalized in the province.

Old Order Mennonites are Canadian citizens and yet have not integrated into the mainstream society. Like other parts of the Anabaptist order, their culture has strong family values that support respectful behavior and a calm environment. The value of learning for girls focuses on domestic tasks. By the end of Grade 8, most girls leave school to work in the home alongside their mothers, or in greenhouses to "bring the money home to Mom and Dad because they have eight mouths to feed, and the parents need help," as one principal put it. By their early 30s, some of them may have six or seven children of their own.

Boys, on the other hand, now sometimes go to high school, and even on to college. These boys are "pushing back from their parents and saying, 'I don't want to be a part of this culture.'" In the meantime, teachers of these students struggle to meet their literacy needs and to help them catch up to their peers.

How can educators respect the faith and family values of this historic culture that, at the same time, has a patriarchal approach to women and girls? How should they respond when members of a religious community restrict educational opportunities of both boys and girls by taking children out of schools for several months each year? What moral issues are involved when parents do not provide support for literacy, and want their young people to enter family life and agricultural work long before the official age for high school completion?

Educators know they can't legally force these parents to send their children to school beyond a certain age (since they would simply migrate to another part of their community in Mexico or other parts of Latin America). Instead, they are adopting creative ways to promote "a generational change in attitudes to education by building trust and relationships with families." For example, some of the schools decided to purchase produce from the local community in their own school lunch programs. One principal described how part of his job was just to hang around the community and talk to people, carry their shopping home for them, and build relationships that might facilitate a generational change in attitudes. He understood that leadership that acknowledges the power of identity requires much more than increasing standardized test scores. This is just one instance of how effective leaders are developing practical strategies for dealing with conflicting intersectionality.

FROM THE FIELD: CATHOLIC VERSUS LGBTQ+ IDENTITY

For many people of religious faith, their first and most important relationship—more important even than with their parents, children, or partners—is between themselves and their God. Whether Muslim, Jewish, Christian, Buddhist, Hindu, or something else, some idea of a relationship to what is divine is a core part of their identity. This can have a history that stretches back more than two millennia and that often overlaps with their ethnicity. The *Torah*, the *Quran*, the *Bible*, and other holy books are read as guides to and reminders of how to be, and how to become, a better person.

Educators who seek to downplay or marginalize these aspects of the human experience that are foundational in their students' lives do so at their peril. Faith identities are real. They must be assigned the same respect and empathy as any other forms of identity.

In many countries, it is hard to imagine how national educational goals and the culture of schools could be defined separately from religious tradition—from the Jewish faith in Israel, Catholicism in Ireland, and the Muslim faith in Islamic countries such as many of the Gulf states, for instance. Despite some governments' efforts and legislative provisions to establish a clear separation between church and state, in practice, issues of religious faith and identity often arise in schools. Even parents who are secular often select schools that are faith-driven, stating that they find in them a sense of moral purpose that is of value for their children.

Officially, Ontario is a secular public system. Nonetheless, 37 of its 72 districts are Catholic. The existence of Catholic schools and school districts as publicly funded institutions goes back to the provisions of the British North America Act in 1867 (section 93) in which education rights held by religious minorities at the time of confederation were legally secured. In this regard, Catholic schools in Ontario bear similarities to the publicly supported Catholic system in Australia. This makes them very different from Catholic schools in the United States or United Kingdom, for example, which rely on private tuition funds for their revenues. They are also different because of the role of language in Canada; 29 of Ontario's Catholic districts are anglophone and 8 are francophone. Finally, even though, in many countries, religion is in the foreground when it comes to identity, in the United States little or no acknowledgment of religion appears in the multicultural or antiracist literature.

One feature of the Ontario Catholic school system is the way that faith permeates the vision, pedagogy, and curriculum content of these districts. Several system leaders said they drew on their religious convictions to promote their students' identity formation. One of them said, "Identity is where we start. That's how we develop a sense of who we are, created in the image and likeness of God." Another leader remarked that "Catholic identity is really a part of who we are. When we do work in identity, we're already grounded in it. The teacher already comes in with the experience of identity being so crucial to who that person is."

Catholic faith was realized in different ways in the districts we studied. One system's leadership team practiced "Christian meditation at the start of meetings." "That's very purposeful and deliberate because it's this idea of just turning off, unplugging, and placing ourselves in the presence of God and in the presence of the creator, and of one another," the director explained. "There is a concept of contemplative practice and a concept of human dignity [that] is the core [of] social teaching. That allows us to enter into relationships from the basis of identity and culture," another system leader noted. A fellow superintendent concurred: "Everybody is created in the image and likeness of God and will be treated with dignity and respect," he said.

Catholic identity meant prayer and communion for some. For others, it involved learning about how harsh life can be for those who are marginalized. In one school, a teacher said, "students learned about what agencies help people who are homeless, who are hungry. I think there's a lot of good, real-life learning there, and the chance to share authentically with the kids."

A social studies teacher in another school made sure his students learned about "all kinds of world issues" that were impacting local communities. Students learned that because of acid mine drainage, "there's not clean drinking water in the lake, which is 30 minutes away. Gold mining is destroying people's homes." A Grade 3 elementary school teacher invited in speakers from homeless shelters and asked students to reflect afterward upon the Gospel preaching that "whatever you do to the least of my brothers, you do to me."

In Ontario's Catholic schools today, identity also means reflecting on where the Catholic faith and its adherents have been flawed or fallen short—especially in relation to the history of the Catholic Church and its role in the oppression of Indigenous peoples. "You have the discussion about that history. That's where we're going with the residential schools, and that's new for Canadians," a district superintendent commented. Another system leader noted how, on a school visit, he had witnessed conversations about residential schools in religion, English, and social studies classes. "You have those conversations about colonialism," he pointed out.

At the same time, although 29 countries have legalized same-sex marriage, the Catholic Church still does not officially recognize it. As publicly funded schools, Ontario's Catholic schools are required to comply with government policy, including policy related to inclusion and sexual orientation. This has been difficult for some Catholic educators to address. The same district leaders who were explicit about their work in acknowledging and celebrating Indigenous identities struggled when it came to how their districts supported LGBTQ+ students. "That's a complicated question and a complicated answer," one leader said, although, in general terms, they would "want to celebrate who you are and your identity," with specific reference to LGBTQ+:

> As a group, do we celebrate that as a Catholic system? No. We have banners for [Indigenous groups], but we're not having banners celebrating *that* identity [saying] "Isn't this wonderful?" We don't do it. Should we? I don't know. I think we've come a long way to really get to where we are, but maybe that would be the evidence that we've really come as far as we need to when we actually could say, "We celebrate kids being gay." We don't.

At the time of our research around 2015–2016, educators in other schools stated that they were asked by Catholic leaders to avoid names for student clubs like *Gay–Straight Alliances* and to opt for other titles like *Diversity Clubs* instead. LGBTQ+ advocates argued that this euphemistic evasion helped perpetuate the continued marginalization of LGBTQ+ youth.

Ontario's Catholic schools have made progress on LGBTQ+ identity issues since our report's publication. For the first time, in 2021, at least eight Catholic districts, including one in our study, approved the flying of the rainbow pride flag in schools every June to promote the inclusion of LGBTQ+ students. One district we studied went further and mandated professional development for all staff that explicitly included support for LGBTQ+ students. One Catholic school superintendent also wrote to the province's Ministry of Education requesting a comprehensive review of all official curriculum materials to ensure they properly addressed issues of identity, including gender diversity.

These developments are responses to continuing changes in the wider culture of Canada and elsewhere toward the LGBTQ+ community. Catholic school leaders have contended with potential government threats to withdraw funding for their schools unless they fully comply with government policy. They have also had to respond to LGBTQ+ activism, such as that from the Ontario Student Trustees' Association, which published an open letter to the leaders of the province's Catholic schools, calling on them to comply with the Accepting Schools Act.[30] Overall, this example of conflicting intersectionality offers hope that activism, persistence, and openness to empathy and learning can yield progress in taking an inclusive stance toward all identities, even in relation to those that had previously been at odds with each other.

> Activism, persistence, and openness to empathy and learning can yield progress in taking an inclusive stance toward all identities.

FROM THE FIELD: HERITAGE CULTURES VERSUS IMMIGRANT IDENTITY

French Canadian and Franco-Ontarian identities, we have shown, have suffered historically from oppression and marginalization. Increasingly, though, traditionally homogeneous Franco-Ontarian culture is also challenged by the existence and inclusion of more international French-speaking students, most of whom are from immigrant families. Some Franco-Ontarian educators admitted that they had found it difficult to include French-speaking students from North Africa, Haiti, and the Middle East without perceived risks to their own imperiled identity.

In our earlier study in 2011, a principal in one francophone school had worried about "white bread parents" who would say that they wanted "a multicultural education and this is exciting, until somebody by the name of Ali or Hassan makes trouble with your kid." Another principal reported a child saying that she didn't like a supply (substitute) teacher "because she's Brown and I don't like Brown people." Educators acknowledged that their schools were changing and that some forms of bigotry that had been hidden in the past were visible now because "we didn't have these kinds of students before." They also seemed eager to talk with students and parents about the value of growing cultural diversity for their schools.

By 2016, in some of the schools, 90% of the students were immigrants. One school had 78 nationalities. The 10 largest sending countries of francophone immigrants to Ontario were Lebanon, Haiti, the Democratic Republic of the Congo, France, Morocco, Mauritius, Algeria, Burundi, Cameroon, and Rwanda. This is an extraordinary array of nations with different histories, cultures, and kinds of spoken French.

Although traditional Franco-Ontarian culture was "declining, older, [and] more rural but undergoing increasing urbanization," educators observed that the French language was now situated in a dynamic global community of "at least 30 countries" and approximately 355 million speakers that could contribute to a cosmopolitan future. However, while Franco-Ontarian schools were experiencing students bringing "greater cultural diversity" with them, these students were not necessarily strengthening Franco-Ontarian culture because "many of them speak a form of French that is different from the French spoken in Ontario." The students used different idioms, had different cultural references, and sometimes spoke a patois that wasn't recognizable to the native Franco-Ontarian students and their parents.

The challenge was to preserve traditional Franco-Ontarian heritage, while at the same time integrating a growing number of immigrants and refugees. The response was to make the students' "entry and inclusion, as well as that of their parents," "a source of dialogue and learning for everyone in daily contact with the school." To take full advantage of this diversity, teachers realized it was not enough to assert traditional Franco-Ontarian identity.

> Right now, for our end-of-the-year concert, we're going to be using the theme of "around the world," and we're trying to pick songs or dances from countries from where the kids are from. We're going to have their families on posters around the stage, so we're planning to incorporate all the different ethnicities in the school and to showcase it. We've also had activities where the parents of

these students would come in, [and] talk with the class about the differences about where they're from. We would show videos of their different countries or different songs, different cultures.

One of the district's consultants described how

there was a lot of talk around Christmas and so on with the little kids. We said, "It might be useful to look at other festivals of light or other festivals to make sure that there's a whole array of different traditions that are talked about." It was taking what they were already doing and looking at ways that we could supplement that to make sure that the school climate was also one in which all the kids feel comfortable learning.

An elementary school principal believed these efforts were appreciated among both traditional and newcomer students: "The children accept differences well at the schools. They're integrated very, very well. The teachers made a conscious effort to make sure our children are integrated and feel good. Not just the new arrivals but all students."

Educators supported their school's endorsement of a global francophone identity that included French speakers from all over the world. One teacher explained:

We have francophonie, which is a francophone activity celebration—so we had our own version of the francophonie, and we celebrate that with the kids, too. That's part of the francophone culture, and our mandate in our school district is to celebrate the francophone culture and language and make it living and authentic for them. It's not something that belongs to the school. It belongs to them.

The identity issues of Franco-Ontarians are not resolved with festivals alone, of course. Public hearings have revealed a concern that "integrating newcomers without many roots in the community (more specifically without any roots in the local Franco-Ontarian community) may dilute feelings of belonging to the community."[31] The conflicting intersection of Franco-Ontarian and immigrant French-speaking identities therefore remains a continuing struggle requiring constant attention, engagement, advocacy, and empathy.

WHERE THE RUBBER MEETS THE ROAD

We have provided three examples of conflicting intersectionality and the complex issues they raise of dignity and respect for different cultures, alongside conforming with universal human rights. There are many other examples, of course, that are not represented in our data. In a world where conflicting intersectionality is abundant, it is important to discuss it openly, and not avoid the topic or change the subject. Patricia Hill Collins describes this as "being centered in one's own experience while being empathetic to the partners in the dialogue."[32]

When Andy served as president of the International Congress for School Effectiveness and Improvement (ICSEI) between 2017 and 2019, he found, in preparing for his role, that some members perceived the organization as being too old and too white. So, making this issue a priority of his leadership platform, he was delighted when the board voted to hold its 2020 congress in Morocco, a predominantly Muslim country—the first time the organization had ever met in Africa. However, when this was announced at the annual general meeting, one outraged member asked, "Why is ICSEI holding congresses in countries where homosexuality is illegal?"

The upcoming congress, Andy and the board realized, presented a situation of conflicting human rights. In being inclusive of race, faith, and the Global South, the organization was also risking the exclusion and safety of gender-identity minorities.

ICSEI responded by developing and publishing an ethics policy on how to approach these issues. It secured assurances about intellectual freedom and basic safety for all members within the Morocco congress. The speaker platform also included presentations on LGBTQ+ issues in schools. Ethics policies like those that ICSEI created can and should inform educational leaders about what to do when dilemmas such as competing human rights must be dealt with so that clear criteria are available to everyone. Learning how to participate in conversations like these should be an explicit part of teachers' and leaders' professional development.

Intersectionality, and especially conflicting intersectionality, is where the rubber of increasing inclusion meets the road of righteous indignation. Addressing, sometimes embracing, and also confronting different kinds of intersectionality must be about more than either celebrating some cultures and traditions or criticizing and even vilifying others.

Addressing, sometimes embracing, and also confronting different kinds of intersectionality must be about more than either celebrating some cultures and traditions or criticizing and even vilifying others.

Working in a knowledgeable, empathetic, and honest way with all forms of intersectionality must be about *engaging* the tensions within and between different kinds of identity and addressing how they might be handled. No group should feel oppressed. No identity, unless it is egregiously immoral, should be overlooked or ignored. We should be wary of simplistically dividing entire groups and all their members into unambiguously privileged oppressors and the unequivocally marginalized and oppressed. While the power dynamics and matrices of oppression and marginalization are real and deserve full attention, simplifying the issues by creating mutually exclusive and hermetically sealed identity categories associated with right and wrong, good and evil, or privileged and marginalized, in immoderate discourses of pride and shame, will do little to advance inclusion, togetherness, or belonging in the end.

There is no such thing as a flawless identity. Diversity is not always an unconditional positive, to be celebrated in food and festivals. If it were, we would lionize white supremacist groups, misogynists and homophobes, and the Flat Earth Society (it really does exist!) simply because they are different.

We must show empathy for the complexity and authenticity of one another's positions. We must respect cultural uniqueness and tradition. At the same time, we must also advocate for the importance of human rights, including the rights of the child. There will sometimes be unavoidable imperfections in what we see and what we want, including our efforts to resolve competing human rights. Wherever we can, we must transcend our differences and work together.

These aspirations are achievable. For decades, working-class women had to fight not only their governments but also their male-dominated working-class trade unions for the right to equal pay, but this issue is now recognized in international labor law. Same-sex marriage that was once prohibited everywhere is now a legally recognized human right, even in overwhelmingly Catholic countries like Ireland, Mexico, Colombia, and France. Intersectional conflicts and tensions can sometimes eventually be overcome. In modern-day democracies, ultimately, they should be.

This chapter has described how teachers are navigating the maze of critical, constructive, and conflicting intersectional identities. In our next, final chapter, we will draw all this together in practical and strategic terms to guide educators and especially educational leaders in how to forge new pathways of identity, equity, and inclusion for the future that do their utmost to bring people together in support of increased inclusion rather than driving them apart.

Notes

1.   Barclay, J., Chadha, G., & Daniel, J. (Producers), & Chadha, G. (Director). (2019). *Blinded by the light* [Film]. Levantine Films.

2.   Manzoor, S. (2008). *Greetings from Bury Park: Race, religion and rock 'n' roll.* Vintage, p. 1.

3.   Manzoor, S. (2019, August 29). My film is bridging cultural divides. This gives me hope in such polarised times. *The Guardian*. https://www.theguardian.com/commentisfree/2019/aug/29/my-film-blinded-by-the-light-memoir-british-pakistani-cinema

4.   Whitman, W. (1993). *Leaves of grass.* Modern Library, p. 113. (Original work published 1855)

5.   Crenshaw, K. (1989). Demarginalizing the intersection of race and sex: A Black feminist critique of antidiscrimination doctrine, feminist theory and antiracist politics. *University of Chicago Legal Forum, 1*(8), 139–167.

6.   Columbia Law School. (2017, June 7). *Kimberlé Crenshaw on intersectionality, more than two decades later* [Interview]. https://www.law.columbia.edu/news/archive/kimberle-crenshaw-intersectionality-more-two-decades-later

7.   Crenshaw, Demarginalizing the intersection of race and sex.

8.   Ibid., quote from p. 140.

9.   Collins, P. H. (2000). *Black feminist thought.* Routledge, p. 26.

10.   Ibid., p. 21.

11.   May, V. M. (2015). *Pursuing intersectionality: Unsettling dominant imaginaries.* Routledge, p. 23.

12.   Braun, L. (2016, June 30). 10 reasons to love Drake for Canada Day. *Toronto Sun*. https://torontosun.com/2016/06/30/10-reasons-to-love-drake-for-canada-day

13.   Drake. (2013). Started from the bottom [Song]. On *Nothing was the same*. Aspire.

14.   Williams, L. (2022, October 16). "Goes against everything I stand for" Alex Scott left in tears over family history. *Express*. https://www.express.co.uk/showbiz/tv-radio/1506885/Alex-Scott-tears-family-history-Who-Do-You-Think-You-Are

15.   Rolle, L., Giardina, A. M., Gerino, E., & Brustia, P. (2018). When intimate partner violence meets same sex couples: A review of same sex intimate partner violence. *Frontiers of Psychology, 9*, 1506. https://doi.org/10.3389/fpsyg.2018.01506

16.   Schubert, F. N. (2009). *Voices of the buffalo soldier: Records, reports, and recollections of military life and service in the west.* University of New Mexico Press.

17.   Bob Marley and the Wailers. (1983). Buffalo soldier [Song]. On *Confrontation*. Tuff Gong; Island.

18.   Smith, R. P. (2018, March 6). How Native American slaveholders complicate the Trail of Tears narrative. *Smithsonian*. https://www.smithsonianmag.com/smithsonian-institution/how-native-american-slaveholders-complicate-trail-tears-narrative-180968339/

19.   Ferguson, D. (2019, May 26). "We can't give in": The Birmingham school on the frontline of anti-LGBTQ protests. *The Guardian*. https://www.theguardian.com/uk-news/2019/may/26/birmingham-anderton-park-primary-muslim-protests-lgbt-teaching-rights

20.   Tiku, N. (2023, March 22). Tech workers claimed caste bias. Now California could make it illegal. *The Washington Post*. https://www.washingtonpost.com/politics/2023/03/22/tech-workers-claimed-caste-bias-now-california-could-make-it-illegal/

21. Owalade, T. (2023, April 15). Racism in Britain is not a black and white issue. It's far more complicated. *The Guardian.* https://www.theguard ian.com/commentisfree/2023/apr/15/racism-in-britain-is-not-a-black-and -white-issue-it-is-far-more-complicated

22. Sharma, S. (2023, April 4). UK's Suella Braverman targets Pakistan-origin men, says "grooming gangs" are abusing white English girls. *Business Today.* https://www.businesstoday.in/latest/world/story/uks-suella-braverman-targets-pakistan-origin-men-says-grooming-gangs-abusing-white-english-girls-375945-2023-04-04

23. Cassidy, J. (2021). *Representations of religion in the Ontario secondary school curriculum* [Unpublished master's thesis]. Faculty of Education, University of Ottawa.

24. Ibid., p. 6.

24. Ibid.

25. Ibid., p. 115.

26. Ibid., p. 118.

27. Taylor, C. (2018). *A secular age.* Harvard University Press.

28. Loewen, R. (2013). *Village among nations: "Canadian" Mennonites in a transnational world, 1916–2006.* University of Toronto Press.

29. Ibid.

30. Ontario Student Trustees' Association. (2022, February 23). *An open letter to the trustees, directors of education and staff of the Ontario Catholic school boards.* https://osta-aeco.org/blog/2022/02/23/addressing-homophobia-in-catholic-education/

31. Barber, K. (2014). *Ontario francophone immigrant profile: Immigration trends and labor outcomes.* Ryerson Centre for Immigration and Settlement. https://www.ryerson.ca/content/dam/rcis/documents/RCIS_MCI_PC_Fellowship_Report_Barber_2014.pdf, p. 16.

32. Collins, P. H. (2000). *Black feminist thought*, p. 265.

CHAPTER 7

Learning to Live Together

"I hope—friend—that you sometimes doubt, too. It's human to doubt."

—From *Monsignor Quixote* by
Graham Greene (1982)

Commitment without doubt is nothing more than zealotry. Doubt without commitment is little other than deconstruction for its own sake. It is when commitment and doubt come together that progress becomes possible.

Commitment and Doubt

Graham Greene is one of the most celebrated authors of the modern novel. In *Monsieur Quixote*, Greene presents a parody of Miguel de Cervantes's classic novel, *Don Quixote*.[1] The plot develops through the interactions between two protagonists: a small town's Catholic priest and communist mayor. At roughly the same time, for entirely different reasons, these two rotund characters find themselves suddenly unemployed in their village. They decide to take a holiday together, cramped in a tiny old car, on a long journey across Spain.

Each man has passionate convictions about Catholicism and Marxism, respectively. In the early days of their journey, they regale each other relentlessly with their competing beliefs. As time passes, a relationship develops, and trust builds between them. Slowly, each of them starts to articulate and share his deepest doubts. The Catholic priest questions the basic existence of God. The Marxist mayor despairs whether the communist revolution will ever happen.

In the end, their journey is an allegory of the relationship between commitment and doubt. The passionate fervor of their moral convictions drives them to argue with each other. But it is their doubts that turn these ideological salvos into genuine conversation and dialogue.

Commitment without doubt is nothing more than zealotry. Doubt without commitment is little other than deconstruction for its own sake. It is when commitment and doubt come together that progress becomes possible. In a world and at a time when identity politics are often tearing us apart, this final chapter is about how to engage both commitment *and* doubt in a shared pursuit of a more inclusive and equitable common good.

Pedagogies of Change

When identities are damaged, everyone suffers. Hiding who we are holds us back in what we can accomplish. We become traitors to ourselves. Disregarding or disrespecting others' identities unleashes anger and frustration. Or it inflicts depression and despair. Relationships become toxic. Groups fail to function. Potential is unrealized, and learning gets lost.

This is economically wasteful. It is also morally unjust. Exclusion creates inequity. Inclusion can start to put things right. It is a first step we can take as educators. But it is barely a beginning.

How can we get greater inclusion without provoking indignation among people who feel that its beneficiaries are getting special treatment? How do we get beyond symbolic apologies for wrongdoings and make substantive restitution by raising taxes, or by drawing from the deep coffers

> When identities are damaged, everyone suffers. Hiding who we are holds us back in what we can accomplish. We become traitors to ourselves.

of governments and religious organizations that have been responsible for historic oppressions?

What can we do to get rich individuals and organizations to redistribute some of their *wealth privilege* not just according to their paternalistic preferences, but through fair taxation, in line with the public good? What are some of the most effective ways to get people to face up to the implications of their *white privilege*, when research evidence and finger wagging isn't working?

How do we address the many examples of *conflicting intersectionality*, where groups and individuals seem to be oppressed and marginalized in some ways, but oppressors and privileged in others? Our book has tried to set out what the issues are. The question now is: *What can be done?*

Experience and research concerning inequity, exclusion, and oppression in relation to people's identities can help us to understand *what* needs to be changed and why. But then we need another body of evidence to guide us in *how* to get people to change for the better, especially when they may be skeptical about the *Age of Identity* and their own involvement in it. Simply making people aware of the evidence or insisting that they alter their ways is not an effective change strategy. This doesn't work with teenagers. It rarely works with adults, either.

We need to combine the kind of evidence and insight we have presented in this book, about *what* needs to be changed, with understandings of *how* people change. Teachers know that no matter how interesting a body of curriculum content is, students won't take it in if it's delivered with bad pedagogies. Learning to change is no different. The history of educational change is littered with failed innovations, broken promises, and ineffective implementation. What can we learn from the literature on successful and unsuccessful approaches to educational change that will enable us to achieve inclusion and end oppression in practice and not just in theory?

Based on our experience as researchers and partners in improvement with schools, districts, governments, and international organizations, the following list summarizes 15 things we have learned about why change often fails.

15 REASONS WHY CHANGE OFTEN FAILS

1. It is imposed and unwanted.
2. It is unclear, unethical, or too vague.
3. It is treated as a separate event, not a long-term process.

4. It does not involve the people most affected by it.

5. It happens too fast for people to cope with.

6. It is too slow and leaves people frustrated and bored.

7. It ignores or amplifies people's feelings of loss that accompany most changes.

8. It does not show what people will gain for themselves by making the change.

9. It does not create, demonstrate, and celebrate early outcomes of success.

10. It does not give educators access to real examples of positive change in practice.

11. It does not involve leaders as committed participants in the change.

12. It is experienced individually, not collaboratively.

13. It does not provide adequate time during the working day to implement it.

14. It provides insufficient coaching support when teachers try out new practices.

15. It provides coaching that is based on compliance rather than learning.

Professional Learning and Development

What happens when we flip these 15 reasons? Successful change requires effective and widespread professional learning and development (PLD). Educators must want to learn and see the point of what they are learning. They must understand what they are learning, deeply and not superficially. They must be able to put what they learn into practice and have time and support to do so, considering everything else they must deal with.

Teachers need to be encouraged by supportive coaches and colleagues, especially when things don't work out at first. They need to feel that failures in practice or using not quite the right words in professional dialogue are occasions for learning, rather than reasons to be patronized or scolded. Like learners of a second language, people who make mistakes when they are learning a professional language of diversity and inclusion need to have their confidence and sense of security built up by being supported for making a positive effort, rather than being made to feel bad about their errors.[2]

Learning Forward, formerly known as the National Staff Development Council, is the largest organization that guides and coordinates professional learning for educators in North America and beyond. Its principles and standards for effective professional learning are a major influence on policies and practices of change in many systems. All these are related to its Equity Practices:

> Educators engage in professional learning that helps them create high-quality learning experiences for all students, *honoring all aspects of identity students bring to the school.* Educators build capacity to *serve the whole child*, deepening their understanding of who their students are and *how their life experiences and identities impact what they need at school* [our italics].[3]

Long-standing findings and guidance on effective PLD have identified certain features as being critical.[4]

FEATURES OF EFFECTIVE PROFESSIONAL LEARNING

- *Evidence-informed.* It does not just use what seems intuitively right or superficially fun. It scrupulously refers to sound research.

- *Collaborative.* It is not mainly based on individual study in conferences or workshops. It promotes collaborative professionalism through team participation, joint planning, and collaborative inquiry.

- *Embedded.* Mostly, it is not packaged into after-school workshops or external conference events. It occurs in teachers' everyday work itself, through practice, coaching, feedback, and experimentation.

- *Continuous.* It does not rely on isolated or episodic workshops or training sessions. It operates sustainably over a long period that involves regular engagements with desired new practices.

Sadly, much of the PLD work related to including all people's identities in the quest to achieve greater equity and to combat exclusion and oppression does not align with these principles of effective PLD. It takes important and worthy ideas about what to change, but then manages their implementation poorly. Changes don't succeed, and sometimes achieve the opposite of what is desired.

One striking example is a group of strategies variously known as anti-bias training, diversity seminars, and antiracist PLD. Almost all the Fortune

500 companies have invested millions of dollars in diversity training. Among 670 U.S. higher education institutions, two thirds offer this kind of training, and 29% of them require it of all new faculty. Yet, according to an extensive literature review by Professors Frank Dobbin and Alexandra Kalev, "hundreds of studies dating back to the 1930s suggest that anti-bias training doesn't reduce bias, alter behavior, or change the workplace."[5] Reporting on their meta-analysis of over 800 companies, they find in their *Harvard Business Review* article that numerous workshops intended to reduce prejudice actually *increased* bias.[6] Compared with control groups, institutions that provided anti-bias training often experienced a decline in desirable and measurable outcomes, such as recruitment and promotion of women and people of color.

The theory of change behind much anti-bias training is to surface stereotypes by, for example, taking self-evaluation tests. These biases are then worked on by group facilitators. Dobbin and Kalev have found that the very act of asking people "to suppress stereotypes tends to reinforce them."[7] It's a bit like telling people not to think about elephants, they say. Once you issue the instruction, it becomes almost impossible to think about anything else. "Tell people they are biased and must change their ways," Dobbin and Kalev write, "and you may light up their biases and worsen their behavior."[8] Pointing out biases may induce feelings of shame among participants. This may satisfy some people's desires for psychological retribution, but "the goal of these programs is to make the workplace more inclusive."[9]

The best way of reducing bias and changing behaviors, Dobbin and Kalev continue, is to ensure that employees of diverse heritages work together as equals on projects that serve the core purposes of their organization. Some activities that aren't even framed as anti-bias initiatives, they say, such as supportive mentoring, turn out to have the biggest payoff in terms of moving members of underrepresented groups into leadership positions.

There's no point trying to address important and needed changes with ineffective change strategies. Remember why change fails. Diversity and anti-bias training will not work if it feels imposed and unwanted. Words beginning with prefixes like *anti*, *de*, *dis*, and *mis* wave huge red flags to people that they will be made to give things up because they are in the wrong. Any training will not work if it mainly emphasizes what people will lose and doesn't demonstrate what people themselves can gain beyond making sacrifices to do the right thing. Working together on improvement is a more effective and inclusive approach.

> The best way of reducing bias and changing behaviors is to ensure that employees of diverse heritages are working together as equals on projects that serve the core purposes of their organization.

Dobbin and Kalev are not alone in condemning the "spectacular failure" of most anti-bias training.[10] Writing in *The Washington Post*, African American anesthesiologist Marilyn Singleton has decried mandated "implicit bias training" that all California physicians must now take every two years for a full 50 hours in order to be fully certified. "Studies are finding that implicit bias training has no effect on its intended targets and might even make matters worse," she notes.[11] "The malignant false assumption that Black people are inherently inferior intellectually has been traded in for the malignant false assumption that White people are inherently racist," she argues.[12]

If we apply the criteria for successful PLD to anti-bias training, we can ask:

- Is the training based on *research evidence*, rather than just personal experiences and moral injunctions?

- Is it truly *collaborative*, or does it rely excessively on outside consultants?

- Is it *embedded* in the workplace, or does it adopt a one-off, checklist approach to avoid litigation and secure certification?

- Is it a *continuous* part of an ongoing organizational commitment or a set of mandated episodic events?

It's time to stop trying to achieve inclusive and participatory ends with exclusionary and imposed means. Guilt and shame are appropriate for acknowledging and correcting past wrongs such as slavery or the cultural genocide of Indigenous peoples. Suppression and compliance are also essential for preventing deliberate acts of wrongdoing. Preventing racist abuse and sexual harassment, for example, certainly requires frameworks of legal prohibition and monitoring. But strategies of guilt, shame, and prohibition are of little or no value in helping people who want to do the right thing to improve and enrich their relationships and practices of inclusion in classrooms, schools, and other organizations. We need to employ successful change strategies instead.

This final chapter identifies five broad approaches that are more likely to secure greater equity and inclusion in action. It draws on relevant research evidence and on examples of effective inclusion and identity work we have outlined in this book.

1. *Twelve guiding principles* steer honest, productive, inclusive, and respectful dialogue about identity and inclusion in our schools and communities.

2. *Three segments of representation, sympathy, and learning* deepen our relationships to others in a circle of interconnection and inclusion.

3. *Protocols* enable controversial subjects to be addressed in ways that will lead to positive and inclusive outcomes.

4. *A "whole school for the whole child" strategy* ties effective inclusion and fulfillment of all identities to the unique diversities of every student.

5. *Self-determined learning* empowers students to direct aspects of their education in ways that demonstrate to their teachers who they are and what they know.

Guiding Principles

If we want to achieve greater inclusion for all our students, we need to use practices that guide professional conversations in ways that benefit all the adults, too. It's no use having workshops that leave good people with bad feelings about themselves and their teaching. It's poor change practice to perseverate on what people are doing wrong, will have to give up, and will lose, rather than on what can be built upon to create better practice together. Being positive about what can be done rather than only criticizing what has already been done and cannot be changed should be the main driver for improvement. Conversations and decision making should bring us together rather than drive us apart. They should engage people in ways that do not belittle them. They should also recognize that all of us are imperfect and that none of us have all the answers.

With these things in mind, we advance 12 principles that can bring about progress for all of us in a world of multiple, intersecting identities.

> It's poor change practice to perseverate on what people are doing wrong, will have to give up, and will lose, rather than on what can be built upon to create better practice together.

12 GUIDING PRINCIPLES TO GUIDE PROFESSIONAL CONVERSATIONS

Sympathy: to feel intensely *with* and not just have empathy *for* the suffering of those who are stigmatized and marginalized

Bravery: to be courageous in standing up for the rights of others, even if it risks unpopularity among peers or with those in positions of power

Solidarity: to bring people into fellowship to share commonalities, explore and enjoy differences, and learn to live in peace together

Dignity: to recognize, in accordance with the Universal Declaration of Human Rights, that "all human beings are born free and equal in dignity and rights" and deserve honor and respect

 Generosity: to value the strengths of others and what they offer, and not let forgivable flaws, occasional errors, or unavoidable imperfections negate their contributions

 Forgiveness: to accept that others will make mistakes in what they say and how they say it and make allowances when they do

 Civility: to manage disagreement with others who have different views about identity issues from us with active listening and human decency

 Humility: to recognize when our egos are getting in the way and to accept that we haven't got it all figured out just yet

 Irony: to not always take ourselves too seriously, but to bring ourselves down a peg or two sometimes with a bit of self-deprecation

 Authenticity: to express oneself fully and freely in a way that does not impinge on other people's ability to express themselves fully and freely, too

 Rationality: to deliberate on identity questions by including logic, science, and reason, in an open-minded respect for evidence

 Practicality: to ensure that what we've worked out ideally must then be anchored in the concrete realities of how we teach and lead and in the realities of our everyday work lives

---

Source: Hand and heart icon by iStock.com/Fourleaflower; sword icon by iStock.com/Ratsanai; solidarity icon by iStock.com/Agate; handshake icon by iStock.com/Turac Novruzova; treasure box icon by iStock.com/matsabe; folded hands icon by iStock.com/Jenny On The Moon; dove icon by iStock.com/PeterSnow; shocked face and winking face icons by iStock.com/Justicon; bow and arrow icon by iStock.com/Vectors Tank; thinking icon by iStock.com/Turac Novruzova; truck icon by iStock.com/SirVectorr.

Figure 7.1   Principles for Guiding Conversations

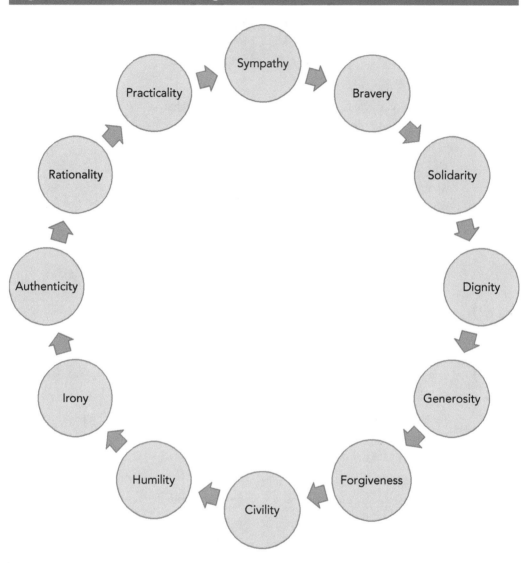

The 12 principles in Figure 7.1 can be clustered into three parts that can be followed in a clockwise direction from the top of the figure.

REFLECTING ON THE 12 PRINCIPLES	
sympathy bravery solidarity	*How shall we commit ourselves to undertake this important work together and persist with it even when things are difficult?*
dignity generosity forgiveness civility humility irony	*How should we conduct ourselves in engaging with and including different, multiple, and complex identities?*
authenticity rationality practicality	*What and who should we involve so we can lead people of different identities toward inclusion effectively?*

First, the principles of sympathy, bravery, and solidarity, from noon to three o'clock, lead us to ask:

How shall we commit ourselves to undertake this important work together and persist with it even when things are difficult?

What will drive us? What is our purpose? How can we truly feel for and feel with those who suffer unnecessarily in our classrooms, schools, and societies? How can we stand up courageously for the lives of others who are marginalized, excluded, and oppressed, even when we are faced with criticism, conflict, and opposition? Who will support us? Who will move with us and help us to keep going when progress is hard? Where will we find solidarity? How can we build it?

Second are the principles of dignity, generosity, forgiveness, civility, humility, and irony. These are about *how to be* and *how to live together* as we engage in hard conversations and deliberations with those around us in relation to equity, inclusion, multiple identities, and the challenges of conflicting intersectionality. These principles, running from three o'clock to eight o'clock, prompt us to inquire:

How should we conduct ourselves in engaging with and including different, multiple, and complex identities?

How can each of us be truly ourselves without being too much of it and overshadowing the identities of others? How are we able to be present in these conversations as self-aware ethical agents who try to do the right thing but who are often also unintentionally implicated in the very exclusions and oppressions we are trying to resolve? How do we remain civil and respect the dignity of others even when we feel we are being unfairly attacked? How can we confront great injustices with a heavy heart yet also have the lightness of being and capacity for self-deprecation that is sometimes necessary to relieve tension, to make ourselves look less austere in disposition, and to avoid coming across as too pious and too perfect? How can we treat others of good intent who sometimes make mistakes in a spirit of generosity and forgiveness?

Last, three culminating principles of authenticity, rationality, and practicality are touchstones of engagement with those around us. These lead us to ask:

What and who should we involve so we can lead people of different identities toward inclusion effectively?

How do we draw honestly and reflectively on our own life experiences to uplift all our students, including those whose identities receive little public recognition or support? Kevin Lamoureux, an Ojibwe/Métis–Ukrainian Canadian scholar of self-defined mixed ancestry, refers to painful experiences, such as his own, that are wrapped up in chains.[13] How do we acknowledge and articulate our own wounds, he asks, and see ourselves as proud and strong survivors, so that we are more easily able to sympathize with the psychic wounds that are experienced by others, instead of tucking away our painful memories of bullying, abuse, or marginalization in shadowy corners of embarrassment and shame?

How do we take responsibility for the privileges and unequal opportunities of our parents' social class, or of our race, or of growing up in a particular generation that may have stacked the deck in our favor, among some of us, compared to others who grew up with fewer assets, in a different time, or with a different background? How do we open ourselves to learning and change when statistical evidence points incontrovertibly to systematic patterns of exclusion and inequality that we have been unaware of, or when neurological and biological science poses uncomfortable challenges to the views that we have come to hold dear about the nature of our own and others' identities? Finally, we must ask, what is practical in terms of the kind of language that we use, which can be understood by everyone and not just academic specialists, in today's schools and classrooms?

Segments of Inclusive Thinking and Action

How do you think about your own identity? How do we engage with the identities of others in their wholeness and complexity, rather than as one-dimensional caricatures that define and divide people as oppressors and oppressed? How do we get to walk in the shoes of others and follow the paths that have defined their lives? As we promote greater inclusion for our students, can we become more inclusive among ourselves? One of the biggest ideas of this book is that identities are complex and shifting. Becoming more inclusive means that we need to find ways to get access to the experiences of very different others.

This section explores an interconnected circle, as depicted in Figure 7.2, to assist with this kind of understanding that contains three segments: *representation*, *sympathy*, and *learning*. Each of them is important in approaching how to connect with, engage with, and support others in pursuit of greater equity and inclusion.

How do we open ourselves to learning and change when statistical evidence points incontrovertibly to systematic patterns of exclusion and inequality that we have been unaware of, or when neurological and biological science poses uncomfortable challenges to the views that we have come to hold dear about the nature of our own and others' identities?

Figure 7.2 Three Segments of Inclusive Thinking and Action

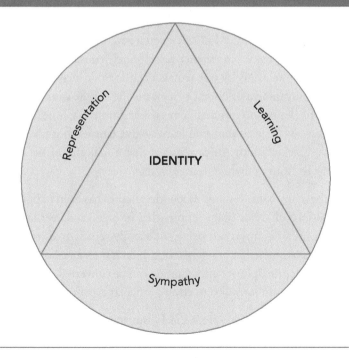

Representation

One way to address how all groups who are affected by a decision, discussion, or direction can be properly included is to ensure that they and their views are represented in a significant way. Representation is about who does and doesn't have a seat at the table, and who is or isn't in the forefront of people's thinking.

Representation is not a new idea. The 1773 Boston Tea Party was triggered by the outraged belief of American colonists that there should be "no taxation without representation." In *Representative Government*, 19th-century British abolitionist John Stuart Mill wrote that "in a really equal democracy, every or any section would be represented."[14] The "virtual blotting-out of the minority," Mill thought, would diminish the range of perspectives available to solve pressing problems.[15] In *On Liberty*, Mill went further and proposed measures to ensure that people with different kinds of lifestyles would be protected by law, as long as their actions and behaviors caused no harm to others. The enemy of a free and open society, he contended, is "the deep slumber of a decided opinion."[16]

Today, governments and societies around the world increasingly accept the importance of representation in public life. In 1991, Argentina passed the world's first national gender quota law, requiring each political party to list a minimum of 30% female candidates for public office.[17] In 2005, Norway introduced a 40% gender quota for the boards of publicly listed companies.[18] Indeed, when we were visiting professors in Norway and proposed a conference panel largely consisting of women, we were gently rebuked by our female dean for not including at least 40% men! Singapore uses quotas to allocate 80% of the country's housing stock to the nation's three major ethnic groups—Chinese, Malay, and Indian—so that citizens will learn to live harmoniously with one another.[19] Cricket South Africa requires that a majority of players on each team be from nonwhite backgrounds.[20]

One of the many contributions of identity politics has been to point out the limitations of "color blind" approaches in organizations that result in marginalized identities not being sufficiently represented in recruitment efforts or leadership positions. But there is then a real danger that this important principle of representation can be converted into bureaucratic checklists and formulae to cover particular types of identity.

Having one representative who is Black, and another who is LGBTQ+, and another who has a physical disability, for example, may not encompass all the identities that are affected and should be considered. What about Brown or East Asian groups, or people with autism spectrum disorder, or people who grew up in working-class families, for example? There are so many different identities that it's hard to know where the list ends. Asking one individual to be a figurehead for all their identities is also too much to ask. There is considerable internal diversity in most identity groups. LGBTQ+ individuals, for instance, may be wealthy or poor. Older African Americans have been critical of tactics used by young Black Lives Matter activists. Indian immigrants to North America who are from the stigmatized Dalit (Sudra) caste sometimes find themselves discriminated against by the upper castes, even in educational institutions, once they settle in their new communities in the United States and Canada.

The point of a positive politics of representation is not to check off all relevant boxes, but to widen contributions beyond a single, dominant, or majority perspective. It is to bring different voices into the room and establish a norm of putting oneself in others' shoes. The most obvious aspect of representation is asking who is in the room. The most essential aspect of it, though, is to always be mindful of who is *not* in the room, and of how their interests and experiences can and should be considered.

In our research for this book, our diverse graduate research team consisted of a gay man, an African American woman, and the white son of a Lutheran preacher. They brought these diverse identities and perspectives to our data collection and analysis processes. As we developed an advanced draft of this book, we also sent copies for feedback to colleagues with a wide range of identities, including Black, Asian, Indigenous, LGBTQ+, the mother of a transgender adult, a specialist in special educational needs, and people who had grown up as part of the white working class. All these forms of representation have widened and deepened our own perspectives on and insights about identity and identities in this book.

Sympathy

The 18th century economist and philosopher Adam Smith asserted that sympathy is the basic emotion of democracy.[21] Feeling what life is like for other people encourages us to take more care of them. We don't talk much about the virtue of sympathy these days. We allocate far more bandwidth to empathy. There's a reason for this.

In his groundbreaking books on emotional intelligence, Daniel Goleman describes empathy as one of five basic aspects of emotional

> The point of a positive politics of representation is not to check off all relevant boxes, but to widen contributions beyond a single, dominant, or majority perspective.

intelligence.[22] Empathy, he argues, is the ability to understand the emotions of others. If we are to find ways to understand people with identities different from our own, empathy, the capacity to know how they feel, is essential.

Empathy embodies the optimistic belief that we don't have to be replicants of someone with another identity to understand them and how they feel. Women can understand men, adults can understand children, extroverts can understand introverts, and people of one race can understand those of another. Empathy is a skill you can learn throughout life, says Goleman, including through precisely constructed training programs. For Yale University professor Marc Brackett, it's simply a question of being able to "understand . . . feelings and determine their source—what experiences actually caused them."[23]

We can also teach empathy in many other ways. Literature, drama, and the arts, for example, give readers and viewers access to other ways of life they could never experience for themselves. They can help us to feel what it's like to be a monarch, an enslaved person, or a convict; to have the motivations of a serial killer or the emotions of a traumatized victim; to live through a war or another significant historical experience; to exist in another culture far away from one's own; or to be part of another generation. Why else would people of many ethnicities read *The Color Purple* or *Wild Swans* if they weren't motivated at least a little by the desire to step into African American or Chinese cultures and all the identities that populate them?[24]

Empathy does not always give a guaranteed connection to the suffering, oppression, and marginalization of others, though. Catfishing uses empathy to extract money from vulnerable people who are desperate for love and attention. Writing in *Scientific American*, Jamil Zaki describes how people can use empathy to manipulate other people. Turn on any commercial TV station, and you'll see empathy being ruthlessly exploited to market products by appealing to viewers' feelings and desires related to envy, lust, gluttony, avarice, and other deadly sins. "Empathic ability is 'value neutral,'" Zaki says, "sometimes helping and other times hurting people."[25]

What can truly help us connect with those whose identities make them prone to marginalization and exclusion is not just empathy, but *sympathy*. This is moving from feeling *for* others, to feeling *with* them. The Merriam-Webster dictionary states that "*sympathy* has been in use since the 16th century." It derives from the Greek *sympathēs*, meaning "having common feelings, sympathetic," formed from *sym* ("with, together with") and *páthos* ("experience, misfortune, emotion,

We don't have to be replicants of someone with another identity to understand them and how they feel.

condition"). *Empathy* has a more recent origin in German philosophy in the early 20th century, and is about "feeling into," rather than "feeling with."[26]

In *The Theory of Moral Sentiments*, Adam Smith argued that "the only way we can get an idea of what someone else is feeling is by thinking about what we would feel if we were in his situation."[27] This involves "imaginatively changing places with the sufferer, thereby coming to conceive what he feels or even to feel what he feels." It requires getting up close to "every little detail of distress that could possibly have occurred to the sufferer."[28]

Smith didn't say how such sympathy can be accomplished. But one way we can develop sympathy for others is by drawing on analogous experiences of our own suffering to arouse fellow feeling, especially when the suffering is not the same. You may not be gay, for instance, but you may be more easily able to empathize with LGBTQ+ individuals who have been bullied if you can connect with having been bullied for another reason. You may not have experienced the hardship of having to flee your homeland to start all over again, but you might have undergone other extreme hardships of your own.

In *On Understanding Emotion*, Norman Denzin describes how *emotional understanding* depends on having the capacity to reach down into the reserves of one's own experiences to connect with the emotions of others.[29] This is different from cognitive understanding, he says. It happens in an instant, in classroom teaching, in chance encounters, or in depictions of famine and war on TV news, for example. When we see a child who has hurt themselves, witness someone being silenced in a meeting, or watch newsreels showing parents weeping for their murdered children, we draw on our own emotional experiences of pain and suffering to engage with what we see. This is how sympathy works when we encounter those who are miserable, depressed, frustrated, or ashamed. We call up our own experiences of these emotions in the past. This is feeling *with*, not just feeling *for*.

Empathy is used much more commonly than sympathy in education and business, partly because of its value-free nature. Empathy can be put to any use, including increasing profits through manipulative marketing techniques. Reports on global competencies by the Organisation for Economic Co-operation and Development (OECD) make regular references to empathy but barely mention sympathy at all. Sympathy—what Smith described as the preeminent moral sentiment—is the emotional foundation of inclusion, equity, and democracy, though. It's time to bring it back.

By itself, sympathy also has limitations. It can all too easily bring on *white savior syndrome*, where pity and compassion lead to others being treated as inferiors who need rescuing or charity. We may feel sorry for the homeless people in the street, for example, but if we just walk on by or even leave them with some of our loose change, this does nothing to improve their basic situation. Both sympathy and representation need something else to transform our conversations about identity and inclusion: learning.

Sympathy without learning can bring on *white savior syndrome,* where pity and compassion lead to others being treated as inferiors who need rescuing or charity.

Learning

The most obvious way to understand something new is to learn it. This is the essence of education. If we believe that understanding diversity can only be achieved by that diversity being represented in the room, then we have given up hope in the power and the promise of learning. Learning is what enables us to understand new things. Learning, awareness, knowledge, and new experience can help us understand different people, cultures, and identities too. If all children can learn, then all adults can, too.

Deliberate learning is what enables people to change, and organizations like schools to change too. Learning moves us to other spaces and higher levels. It creates new awareness, skills, and knowledge. All learning brings about change. And little positive change happens without learning. Learning is the key to unlocking our understanding of our own and other people's identities.

While we were pursuing our collaborative research in Canada, we were also supporting the development of a network of 35 schools in the U.S. Pacific Northwest that were trying to improve student engagement among poor and marginalized student populations. At first, some of the teachers who had been conscripted into the network by their administrators were skeptical about what the project could do for them, given the kinds of children and communities they were working with.

"I teach dirtbag kids from dirtbag parents," one teacher said, as an aside, after an orientation session. When her peers invited her to say more, she shared her frustrations about students who attended class irregularly, who were surly and disruptive when they did come, and whose parents were strung out on crystal meth narcotics. By the end of the evening, though, she had not only been made to feel she had been heard. She had also received some practical ideas about how to help these students succeed. Through subsequent meetings of the network, she grew into a teacher leader. She testified to her own transformed views about what her own students could and did achieve, and she was among the first to take on additional tasks to support her colleagues. Through both informal and formal learning within this network, her identity as a teacher was transformed from embittered outsider to proud professional. A fundamental part of this was that she learned to see her students' identities differently too—no longer as a collection of deficits but, notwithstanding the significant challenges they faced, as a big bundle of assets too.

If this kind of learning can transform people's stereotypes about poverty, it can change minds about race, disability, sexuality, and other formerly stigmatized forms of identity too. The prize-winning film *The Best of Enemies* captures the transformation of former Ku Klux Klansman Claiborne P. Ellis into a committed racial justice advocate.[30] Black community activist Ann Atwater, who Ellis had previously "hated with a purple passion," surprised him by working with tact and dignity when they were both elected to their local school committee. Using a protocol called a *charette* that was based on the pioneering work of social psychologist Kurt Lewin, Ellis and Atwater learned that they both shared common experiences with poverty when they were growing up in the U.S. rural South. Due to this combination of learning combined with sympathy arising out of their experiences of marginalization, Ellis underwent a complete 180-degree turnaround. He disowned his racist past and became a champion of school integration in his community.

Learning does not solve everything, of course. In the classic movie *Groundhog Day*, the protagonist, played by Bill Murray, has to figure out how to live the same day over and over again.[31] At one point he turns to learning as his strategy. He learns to sculpt ice, speak fluent French, play virtuoso piano, and save the life of a diner by performing the Heimlich maneuver. It's impressive. But the only reason he does it is to get the woman of his dreams. Once he achieves his goal, he is left feeling shallow and inauthentic: a man with no identity except for a bag of clever tricks.

Learning without sympathy will do nothing for inclusion in and of itself. Psychopaths can be good at learning. So can confidence tricksters. Sympathy with learning, though, can open up solutions to exclusion and injustice. When representation is also factored in, these solutions can lead to empowering and collaborative action, too.

REFLECTIONS ON REPRESENTATION, SYMPATHY, AND LEARNING

- *Who is and who is not in the room when educators make important decisions?*

- *How can we reach down honestly and courageously into our own wounded experiences of suffering and marginalization so as to empathize and sympathize with different kinds of suffering among others?*

- *How can we pursue learning to improve our understanding of prejudices and exclusions that have adversely affected others and increase our awareness of strategies that can successfully overcome them?*

Conclusion: Segments of Inclusive Thinking and Action

Sympathy with *learning* that moves into action should lead to inclusion and belonging. Widening the conversation through greater *representation* will expand and deepen people's perspectives and the possibilities for equitable and inclusive solutions to the problems we face. Representation, sympathy, and learning are interrelated and intersecting segments of thinking and action that can enable us to understand, engage with, and advocate for others who have identities that are different from ours.

Protocols for Dialogue

Understanding and working with others who are different from us, and conducting dialogue in ways that are respectful and productive, requires more than acts of will and goodwill. It requires protocols to guide difficult conversations. In ancient Greek, the term *protokollon* referred to the first sheet of a book written on papyrus that provided a table of contents. Over the centuries the term has evolved to indicate a recommended code of conduct. Frederick Forsyth's spy thriller *The Fourth Protocol*, for example, is about the breach of a fictional protocol during the Cold War that was designed to guide the sensitive management of nuclear nonproliferation agreements.[32] Today, professionals often use protocols to structure conversations on sensitive topics that can be hard to deal with in an informal or improvised way.

Andy's research and book with Michael O'Connor describes *collaborative professionalism* as a combination of two complementary elements:

- *Solidarity* of relationships of mutual support in a professional community

- *Solidity* of strategies and protocols that can ensure talk leads to effective action, and that enable necessary conversations to take place about difficult issues such as providing critical feedback on classroom teaching, for example[33]

The point of a protocol is to strengthen relationships by protecting people from the likelihood of emotional outbursts and wounded feelings.

The same principles apply to the use of protocols for conducting challenging conversations about diversity and inclusion. One example of how this can be done is inscribed in the British "Chatham House Rule." Chatham House is the home of an international think tank on global policy affairs, based in London. Its most famous rule, known among policy makers around the world, reads as follows:

> When a meeting, or part thereof, is held under the Chatham House Rule, participants are free to use the information received, but neither the identity nor the affiliation of the speaker(s), nor that of any other participant, may be revealed.[34]

The Chatham House Rule is designed to "create a trusted environment to understand and resolve complex problems."[35] Its guiding spirit is "share the information you receive, but do not reveal the identity of who said it."[36] The ARC Education Project that Andy cofounded uses the Chatham House Rule when ministers and senior education officials from different countries meet to solve complex policy problems together.[37]

Other protocols have been developed for guiding what are variously called hard, courageous, or challenging conversations about race and other potentially divisive issues. For instance, Glenn Singleton's Courageous Conversation protocol asks participants to stay engaged throughout, not fall into silence when they feel threatened, and to explore the existence and reasons for any silence that does occur together.[38] It legitimizes and even encourages discomfort and cognitive dissonance, where what is being heard may run contrary to people's long-held beliefs and self-interests. It encourages openness and honesty by removing fear of punitive consequences, and it discourages moves toward premature closure or indeed any kind of closure at all.

In mindful teacher seminars with Boston public school teachers, Dennis has used a protocol originally developed by the U.S. Coalition of Essential Schools network to guide discussions that surface difficult dilemmas and conflicts.[39] The dilemmas are provocative, to say the least. For example:

- What should a teacher do when white students in their class receive all kinds of special services and supports for learning

The point of a protocol is to strengthen relationships by protecting people from the likelihood of emotional outbursts and wounded feelings.

difficulties, but students of color don't get the same assistance because their parents are unsure how to navigate the system?

- What should a white female teacher do when her Black male principal chastises her for teaching an interdisciplinary curriculum unit on the civil rights movement, because he is concerned it will divert instruction away from test preparation?

The protocol enables teachers to work through dilemmas of this kind together. One of its great assets is that it provides a solution in a limited time, since it can be completed in an hour.

Protocols have different value for different purposes. There are many to choose from, including Indigenous protocols of talking circles that predate many others.[40] There isn't one magic protocol that overrides all others. No one has the ultimate answer when it comes to working on identity and inclusion today. This applies to protocols, too.

The Whole School for the Whole Child

When people are only able to participate in society by suppressing essential parts of their identities, and when they have to play roles that they feel are false and forced, they are living the lie of the "divided self." The *Age of Achievement and Effort* required divided selves. It commanded: "Put away your identities, however oppressed and marginalized they might be, and focus on measurable results!"

> The antidote to the divided self in education is *the whole child* taught by whole teachers in whole schools.

The antidote to the divided self in education is *the whole child* taught by whole teachers in whole schools. Indigenous knowledge systems promote child development as a holistic way of being.[41] Montessori, Dewey, Froebel, and the progressive educational movements of the 1920s and 1930s, then 1960s and 1970s, in the United States and United Kingdom, we have seen, also expressed whole-child aspirations in their different ways.

But including and responding to whole children with multiple identities, like the former boy soldier Ishmael Beah, introduced in Chapter 5, can't fall on the shoulders of superhuman individual educators who are expected to be omniscient about all the cultures and identities of all their children. It takes a whole school to raise a whole child.

Between 2019 and 2023, Andy and his University of Ottawa colleague Professor Jess Whitley conducted a developmental evaluation of the

Canadian province of Nova Scotia's sophisticated inclusion strategy. This impressive policy encompasses many kinds of minoritized students such as students with special needs, those with African Nova Scotian or Indigenous identities, and students in rural poor environments. The project administered a survey to school administrators about their efforts to achieve implementation. As illustrated in Figure 7.3, the second-best predictor of successful implementation was how well administrators established "opportunities for teachers to collaborate and dialogue about the needs of their students and themselves."[42] The top predictor of successful implementation was collaboration among administrators *across* schools. In other words, the complex practice of inclusion was most likely to get figured out when educators got down to doing this together.

Figure 7.3   Relationships Between Educators' Collaboration and Successful Inclusion

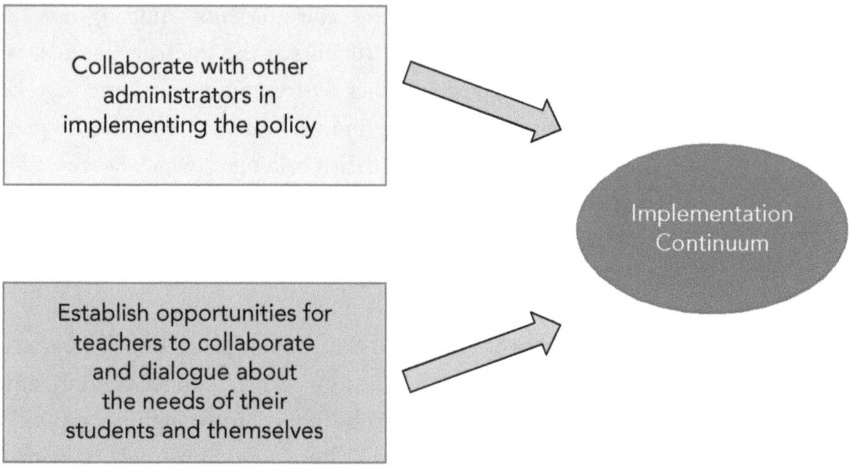

In practice, collaboration in an inclusive educational environment has often come to mean a series of support teams and three levels or tiers of intervention—from in-class instruction through to separate forms of provision for parts of the day that involve working with specialists. But Nayo Upshaw, an African Nova Scotian vice principal at Springhill Junior Senior High School in Springhill, Nova Scotia, described how there is so much more to inclusion and identity than this. All educators are responsible for all the kids, pretty much. Here's one strategy she used:

> Last year, we gave every teacher 10 or 15 cards. None of them were students that they taught. They had to fill out those cards for every student—their name, something they're interested in, where do they live? So, they can get a chance to know other students they don't teach. Because they're all our kids, right?

More sophisticated than this exercise was how the school responded to students who were struggling. The school's collaborative structures and processes that wrapped around such students involved "centering the student, and then everything else is around them so they are really finding out who they are, and what do they bring to the table, and then you're teaching around them."

She went on to describe how the school responded to various vulnerable students who had been affected by the COVID-19 pandemic. "We looked at our 10 most vulnerable students—putting our Indigenous and African Nova Scotian students at the forefront because we already know they're behind and they're struggling. We come together during a student support meeting, and we look at a template we put together, which identifies 'what are their challenges, what's working,'" she said. Then they looked at what multitiered student supports were already being provided in each of the three tiers. If these were still not improving matters, then they asked,

> What are the things we can be doing, additionally, because there's something that's not working? Did we not implement it right? Does it need to be looked at through a trauma-informed lens? Do we not have enough connection with home? What are the issues? It's essentially a template that we came up with that's super, super simple and has 10–15 points. All teachers and support staff connected to that student fill out the template during a support team meeting for that student. We fill out that form together, we put a two-week plan in place with home, and then we come back at the end of that two weeks. We have a Teacher Support Team for all 10 of those kids and we say, "OK, who can we take off this vulnerable list now?" And then we look at what additional supports we need to put in place, because we know their journey doesn't end at those two weeks.

Here, identity, equity and inclusion are not being discussed in the abstract, or in relation to a general policy. Instead, educators with different perspectives do joint work, in action, focused on improving the learning and well-being of individual children. They do this as a strong and committed community, using clear structures and protocols to advance the purposes of full inclusion.

These structures and cultures of educational support exemplify the core features of effective PLD.

- *They are evidence-informed*: aligned with the research evidence on collaborative professionalism. They are also rooted in rich data about the students in question.

- *They are collaborative*: in line with the project's data as well as with the wider literature on effective collaboration that supports inclusion.

- *They are embedded*: an integral part of the everyday work that educators are doing, not an addition to or a departure from that work.

- *They are continuous*: occurring regularly and repeatedly until each student improves their learning or well-being.

Guiding principles and protocols are important for talking about complex and controversial educational matters in the *Age of Identity*. At the end of the day, though, nothing beats grounding this collaborative work in the lives, opportunities, and futures of actual children in real schools.

Self-Determined Learning

Trying to know everything about everybody, all at once, is exhausting. Even doing this together, within a culture of collaborative professionalism, requires immense amounts of time, effort, and resources. But there is one more way to make the *Age of Identity* easier to master. Instead of trying to figure out everything we all know about our students, we can flip the culture and the system, and let students take the lead in telling and showing us all about themselves. After all, no one knows us better than ourselves.

If you are a teacher, think for a moment about your own identity. Would you prefer the administrative team in your school or your district to draw together the knowledge of everyone who has ever worked with you, including your colleagues, so they can then decide what's best

> Instead of trying to figure out everything we all know about our students, we can flip the culture and the system, and let students take the lead in telling and showing us all about themselves.

for you and what kinds of support they need to provide? Wouldn't it be more respectful and effective if they simply asked you directly, or let you show who you are and what you are capable of, through your practice? It's no different for students, or for anybody else, for that matter.

As our book was going to press, Andy interviewed educators in one of the 41 schools on a play-based learning project that he co-directs with Trista Hollweck. Four years earlier, the school's principal had visited an innovative school in another part of Canada. He came back believing that his own school was ill suited to prepare its students for the knowledge and skills they needed to be successful and to thrive in a rapidly changing world.

The principal then set about introducing several innovations. One of these, that he adapted from his school visit, was called *The Genius Hour*—an innovation originally stemming from policies in Google of encouraging employees to devote 20% of their time to projects of interest to them.[43] For one hour a week, students could pursue their own passion project that they picked, and then strive to become a genius in it. One girl made her own solar panel that could contribute to heating her chicken coop after hatching chicks at school. A high school boy designed and built his own guitar from a recycled church pew, having to master mathematics and the physics of sound.

Some teachers were skeptical at first, the principal recalled. They gave sarcastic names to some of the projects. The Genius Hour was dubbed *The Jesus Hour*, for example, out of disdain for the chaos the initiative brought on with so many things happening at once.

Andy asked what changed their minds. It was simple, the principal responded. They were astonished at what their students accomplished. The students showed who they were and what they could do in ways that went far beyond teachers' prior knowledge of them. The *principal* didn't change teachers' minds. The *students* did.

This is an example of what University of Kansas professors Michael Wehmeyer and Yong Zhao call *self-determined learning*.[44] Here, young people don't only regulate their own learning. They decide on and develop it themselves. Teachers get to know who their students are by witnessing what they can do and by talking about it with them, not just when they have finished, but as students are guided and supported through the whole process. The more we flip learning from the teacher running everything, to the student taking the lead, for at least some of the time—in this case just one hour a week—the more that identity issues are no longer a matter of forensic discovery by the adults. Instead, they become a matter of transparent declaration by every student.

INTEGRATING IDENTITIES AND BUILDING BELONGING

All of us have multiple identities. Identities aren't just issues for other people. They matter for everyone. Yet identity issues are tearing people apart. We seem to be locked in a war of all against all, in which our separate identities are marking us out as irreconcilable enemies. White against Black, traditional feminists against transgender activists, nationalists against immigrants, Millenials against Baby Boomers, wars on woke, cancel cultures, and still more besides—all these things are setting people against each other and distracting them from dealing with a world that is falling into economic, environmental, and ethical ruin.

In the economics of scarce attention in schools and school boards, more needs to be done to address the brutal realities of declining school budgets, inadequate teachers' salaries, and continuing educational inequalities, as well as the constricting effects of too much testing, the predatory impact of private companies on children's learning, the dangers of excessive screen time, and the increasing threats of gun violence in U.S. schools and communities. Heated arguments about some of the intricacies of identity politics, concerning pronouns, bathrooms, and nontraditional characters in children's books, for example, can, and indeed sometimes are meant to, distract us from the more systemic causes of inequity and exclusion.

People should be referred to by whatever nouns and pronouns they wish. Like the deceased rock singer Prince, if we wanted, we could call ourselves the professors formerly known as Dennis and Andy. They're our identities, after all. Chosen pronouns are no different. Books should reflect the changing identity landscape of today. It's not 1965 anymore. All children will benefit from having better bathrooms. We need to get these things off the table so we can concentrate on the massive forces and sources of power and inequity that are harming our public schools and damaging many young people's lives.

It's time to stop running from the storm. It's time to be a buffalo—to turn around and face it. Let's shift from arguments that are motivated by outrage and indignation, to conversations that are driven by the desire for greater inclusion. In the words of UNESCO's *Delors Report*, the biggest priority now is to learn to live together.[45] We cannot do that with narratives of change that condemn us to exist in opposition and apart.

To move forward positively and inclusively, we need to cherish the value of both commitment and doubt and to acknowledge the importance of establishing a dynamic relationship between them.

We need to *commit* to identity being a fundamental part of all human and child development. Identity is not only about ethnicities, sexualities, and nationalities. It involves all of us. Self and identity development is as important as cognitive learning and achievement for everyone. Child and adolescent development must be a fundamental part of everything that educators do. Child development isn't the same for all children, in all cultures, at all times, of course. But this is no reason to ignore children's development and the stages through which it passes. The *Age of Achievement and Effort* expunged the identity and self-development agenda from educational systems all over the world. In the *Age of Identity*, it's time once again to educate young people as human beings, rather than mainly as academic performers.

We must also *commit* to ending the oppressions and exclusions of people with certain kinds of identities. In the specter of the *divided self*, people have had to deny their feelings and present inauthentic versions of themselves. *Stigma* has driven people into developing complicated, tortuous, and sometimes self-defeating strategies to manage their spoiled identities that block their capacity for accomplishment and fulfillment.

The antidote to the divided, stigmatized self is an integrated identity, where people are proud to be who they are and feel able to develop a sense of belonging to something bigger than themselves. Identity development is central to the process of education—one in which teachers need to play a full and positive part.

Identities are neither simple nor singular, though. They are complex and multifaceted. Commitment must not lead us into false certainties about our own or others' identities. All of us are many things, not just one. We are multitudes. We must resist the temptation to pigeonhole people into one-dimensional master statuses of race, creed, privilege, marginalization, or any other label that will only lead into cul-de-sacs of stereotypes and checklists. Erving Goffman complained about it. The OECD strongly advises against it. We must see people through lenses of subtlety and complexity, not overconfidence and false certainty. To do this, alongside fervent commitment to doing the right thing, we must entertain doubt about the best ways to proceed.

It is doubt and curiosity, not unswerving certainty, that enables us to see and respond to the many sides of the likes of Ishmael Beah as someone who is much more than being Black or African or a victim of post-traumatic stress, for instance. It is doubt and curiosity that should prompt us to see that a marginalized white boy is not having the same challenges as an excluded Black boy who may also be gay or an undocumented immigrant, for example. When private schools celebrate their diversity, are they using the presence of gender-based and ethnocultural diversity to gloss over the absence of economic or social class diversity? Are upper-middle-class women more, or less, marginalized than impoverished or homeless white men? If there are many ways of being Black or Brown, from socially conservative to politically radical, what should be done about representations of color in educational decision-making or policy-making groups? And how do we accord dignity to and provide inclusion for members of religious and cultural minorities, when powerful male leaders of those groups do not accord equal dignity or inclusion to women or to LGBTQ+ individuals?

Commitment makes us do something about oppression and exclusion. Doubt steers us away from simplistic and excessively certain ways of understanding and responding to it. Nonetheless, doubt alone can condemn us to a state of mental paralysis.[46] In the end, the best response to doubt is action.

It is in this spirit that this final chapter has set out practical strategies that can enable us to understand and engage with one another's identities. This can help us forge some sort of *collective* identity, rather than merely settling for an assortment of *collected* identities. The point of all this is to recognize and include everyone's individual and cultural uniqueness, without giving up hope for or commitment to a transcendent and nonoppressive common good.

The *opportunity* is to nourish our students' evolving senses of self in ways that strengthen their confidence, awaken their curiosity, and cultivate their sensitivity toward others. The *obligation* is to recognize that some identities have been egregiously stigmatized and damaged.

Educators today have both a precious *opportunity* and a daunting moral *obligation*. The *opportunity* is to nourish our students' evolving senses of self in ways that strengthen their confidence, awaken their curiosity, and cultivate their sensitivity toward others. The *obligation* is to recognize that some identities have been egregiously stigmatized and damaged. It is symbolic restoration and material reparation rather than moralizing acts of retribution that will offer the greatest chances of moving forward into a more inclusive world together.

Leadership for inclusive identity is about ensuring that learning triumphs over ignorance, that what is true prevails over what is false, and that what is often essential for some groups—from getting better bathrooms, to greater cultural responsiveness, to fewer incidences of bullying, to more time learning outdoors—is usually good for everyone. Try as we might, we can't escape and mustn't seek to deny our identities. That's not just an *existential reality*. It's an *educational necessity* that should drive all our efforts for greater equity and inclusion in all the years to come.

Notes

1. Greene, G. (1982). *Monsignor Quixote*. Penguin, p. 41.
2. See Dalley, P. (2018, April). *Former des locuteurs et des locutrices confiants: De la théorie à la pratique*. Université d'Ottawa, Faculty of Education, p. 3; Fédération de la Jeunesse Canadienne-Française. (2023). *National strategy for linguistic security*. https://snsl.ca/wp-content/uploads/2020/03/FJCF_2020_SNSL_StrategyDocument_EN_VF_RGB.pdf
3. Learning Forward. (2023). *Equity Practices*. https://standards.learningforward.org/standards-for-professional-learning/rigorous-content-for-each-learner/equity-practices/
4. For example, read Darling-Hammond, L., & McLaughlin, M. W. (1995). Policies that support professional development in an era of reform. *Phi Delta Kappan*, *76*(8), 597–604.
5. Dobbin, F., & Kalev, A. (2018). Why doesn't diversity training work? *Anthropology Now*, *10*(2), 48–55, quote from p. 48.
6. Dobbin, F., & Kalev, A. (2016, July–August). Why diversity programs fail and what works better. *Harvard Business Review*, *94*(7). https://hbr.org/2016/07/why-diversity-programs-fail
7. Dobbin & Kalev, Why doesn't diversity training work?, quote from p. 50.
8. Dobbin, F., & Kalev, A. (2022). *Getting to diversity: What works and what doesn't*. Harvard University Press, p. 16.

9. Ibid.

10. Ibid., p. 11.

11. Singleton, M. (2023, February 22). I'm a Black physician, and I'm appalled by mandated implicit bias training. *The Washington Post.* https://www.washingtonpost .com/opinions/2023/02/22/california-doctor-implicit-bias-training-harmful/

12. Ibid.

13. Lamoureux, K. (2023, February 22). *Ensouling our schools* [Webinar]. Presentation for the High-Performance Leadership Program of the Ontario Catholic School Boards.

14. Mill, J. S. (1975). *Three essays.* Oxford University Press, p. 248.

15. Ibid., p. 252.

16. Mill, J. S. (2015). *On liberty, utilitarianism, and other essays.* Oxford University Press, p. 43.

17. Franceschet, S., & Piscopo, J. M. (2008). Gender quotas and women's substantive representation: Lessons from Argentina. *Politics and Gender, 4*(3), 393–425.

18. Ahern, K. R., & Dittmar, A. K. (2012). The changing of the boards: The impact on firm valuation of mandated female board representation. *The Quarterly Journal of Economics, 127*(1), 137–191.

19. Yap, Y. (2022, May 10). Racial residential patterns in Singapore: What happens after the implementation of racial quotas in public housing? *Current Sociology.* Advance online publication. https://journals.sagepub.com/doi/10.1177/00113 921221093096

20. Mnyanda, S. (2016, April 29). Imposing racial quotas is a vital step forward for South African sport. *The Guardian.* https://www.theguardian.com/world/2016/ apr/29/south-africa-racial-quotas-sport-rugby-springboks-cricket

21. Smith, A. (2017). *The theory of moral sentiments.* Grand Central.

22. Goleman, D. (1995). *Emotional intelligence: Why it can matter more than IQ.* Bantam; Goleman, D. (1998). *Working with emotional intelligence.* Bantam.

23. Brackett, M. (2019). *Permission to feel: The power of emotional intelligence to achieve well-being and success.* Celadon, p. 19.

24. Walker, A. (2019). *The color purple.* Penguin. (Original work published 1982); Chang, J. (2003). *Wild swans: Three daughters of China.* Touchstone.

25. Zaki, J. (2013, November 7). Using empathy to use people. *Scientific American.* https://blogs.scientificamerican.com/moral-universe/using-empathy-to-use -people-emotional-intelligence-and-manipulation/

26. Merriam-Webster. (2023). *What's the difference between "sympathy" and "empathy"?* https://www.merriam-webster.com/words-at-play/sympathy-empathy-difference

27. Smith, *Theory of moral sentiments*, p. 1.

28. Ibid.

29. Denzin, N. (1984). *On understanding emotion.* Jossey-Bass.

30. Strong, D., Bernstein, F., Berenson, M., Bisssell, R., Telson, D., Maguire, T., Plouffe, M. (Producers), & Bissell, R. (Director). (2019). *The best of enemies* [Film]. Astute Films.

31. Albert, T., Ramis, H. (Producers), & Ramis, H. (Director). (1993). *Groundhog day* [Film]. Columbia Pictures.

32. Forsyth, F. (1984). *The fourth protocol.* Vintage.

33. Hargreaves, A., & O'Connor, M. (2018). *Collaborative professionalism: When teaching together means learning for all.* Corwin.

34. Chatham House. (2023). *Chatham House rule.* https://www.chathamhouse.org/about-us/chatham-house-rule#:~:text=The%20Rule%20reads%20as%20follows,other%20participant%2C%20may%20be%20revealed

35. Ibid.

36. Ibid.

37. The ARC Education Project can be accessed at www.atrico.org.

38. Singleton, G. (2022). *Courageous conversations about race.* Corwin.

39. Shirley, D., & MacDonald, E. (2016). *The mindful teacher.* Teachers College Press.

40. On Indigenous talking circles, go to http://firstnationspedagogy.ca/circletalks.html.

41. Blackstock, C. (2011). The emergence of the breath of life theory. *Journal of Social Work and Ethics, 8*(1), 1–16. https://jswve.org/download/2011-1/spr11-blackstock-Emergence-breath-of-life-theory.pdf

42. Whitley, J., Hargreaves, A., Leslie, L., Collins, A., & Arsenault, A. (2023). *Interim report II: Developmental evaluation of the implementation of the Nova Scotia inclusive education policy.* University of Ottawa.

43. See Davis, V. (2022, February 18). Using Genius Hour projects to help students find meaning. *Edutopia.* https://www.edutopia.org/article/using-genius-hour-projects-help-students-find-meaning/

44. Wehmeyer, M., & Zhao, Y. (2020). *Teaching students to become self-determined learners.* ASCD.

45. International Commission on Education for the Twenty-First Century. (1996). *Learning: The treasure within.* United Nations Educational, Scientific and Cultural Organization.

46. French philosopher René Descartes described the danger of excessive doubt in Descartes, R. (1980). *Discourse on method and meditations on first philosophy.* Hackett. (Original work published 1637)

Acknowledgments

We wish to express our gratitude to the many people who engaged with our research on the *Age of Identity* for this book. Michael O'Keefe and Michelle Forge led the Council of Ontario Directors of Education (CODE) Consortium for System Leadership and Innovation that invited us to study the 10 school districts that were collaborating together. They also provided excellent feedback on a draft of this book. Mark D'Angelo, Chris Bacon, and Shaneé Washington joined us in conducting the field research, and we benefitted from the many probing conversations and spirited debates that contributed to the final technical report. Danette Parsley led the Northwest Rural Innovation and Student Engagement network of 35 remote rural schools with which we were honored to work, and which informed some of our most important thinking in this book. Jess Whitley led the development evaluation of Nova Scotia's inclusion strategy with Andy, and she provided thorough comments on an earlier version of this work.

We would like to thank the many other colleagues who also read drafts of the book, and who responded with comments and questions that greatly strengthened this final version. In alphabetical order, they are Paul Armstrong, Phyllis Dalley, Tom D'Amico, Marlen Faannessen, Dean Fink, Ahrum Jeon, Sajani Karunaweera, John Malloy, Norah Marsh, Cathy Montreuil, and Nicola Ngarewa. In addition to providing feedback on a draft of our manuscript, Sajani Karunaweera contributed to the two case descriptions of the schools involved in the Canadian Playful Schools Network.

Finally, we deeply appreciate the support of our families and friends—too numerous to name here—over the many years that we have been working together. This is the fifth book we have written together, and their belief in what we have to say has meant the world to us.

Sections of this book have drawn on and appeared, in part, in the following writings that also include details of our research methodology.

Hargreaves, A. (2020). Class matters: Socio-economic inequality and education. *Education Canada*, *60*(4), 12–14.

Hargreaves, A. (2020). Large-scale assessments and their effects: The case of mid-stakes tests in Ontario. *Journal of Educational Change*, *21*(3), 393–420.

Hargreaves, A., & Shirley, D. (2020). Leading from the middle: Its nature, origins, and impact. *Journal of Professional Capital and Community*, *5*(1), 92–114.

Hargreaves, A., & Shirley, D. (2021). Leadership, identity, and intersectionality. In D. M. Netolicky (Ed.), *Future alternatives for educational leadership: Diversity, inclusion, equity, and democracy* (pp. 111–125). Routledge.

Shirley, D., Hargreaves, A., & Wangia, S. (2020). The sustainability and unsustainability of educators' well-being. *Teaching and Teacher Education*, *92*, 1–12.

Index

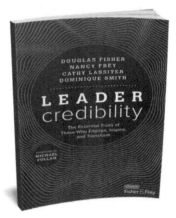

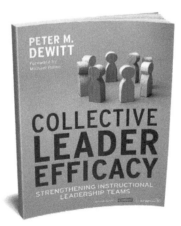
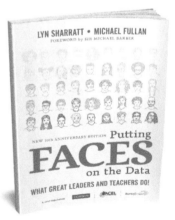

Complement your learning journey with **free resources from Corwin!**

WEBINARS

Listen and interact with education excerpts for an hour of professional learning to gain practical tools and evidence-based strategies—and maybe win some free books!

LEADERS COACHING LEADERS PODCAST

Join Peter DeWitt and his guests as they discuss evidence-based approaches for tackling pressing topics like equity, SEL, burnout, assessment, interrupted formal learning, school administration, and more.

CORWIN CONNECT

Read and engage with us on our blog about the latest in education and professional development.

SAMPLE CONTENT

Did you know you can download sample content from almost every Corwin book on our website? Go to corwin.com/resources for tools you and your staff can use right away!

CORWIN

CORWIN

A Sage Company

CORWIN HAS ONE MISSION: to enhance education through intentional professional learning.

We build long-term relationships with our authors, educators, clients, and associations who partner with us to develop and continuously improve the best evidence-based practices that establish and support lifelong learning.